At Issue

Should Junk Food Be Sold in Schools?

Other Books in the At Issue Series:

At Issue

Should Junk Food Be Sold in Schools?

Norah Piehl, Book Editor

GREENHAVEN PRESS
A part of Gale, Cengage Learning

GALE
CENGAGE Learning

Detroit • New York • San Francisco • New Haven, Conn • Waterville, Maine • London

Christine Nasso, *Publisher*
Elizabeth Des Chenes, *Managing Editor*

© 2011 Greenhaven Press, a part of Gale, Cengage Learning.

Gale and Greenhaven Press are registered trademarks used herein under license.

For more information, contact:
Greenhaven Press
27500 Drake Rd.
Farmington Hills, MI 48331-3535
Or you can visit our Internet site at gale.cengage.com

For product information and technology assistance, contact us at

Gale Customer Support, 1-800-877-4253
For permission to use material from this text or product, submit all requests online at www.cengage.com/permissions

Further permissions questions can be emailed to permissionrequest@cengage.com

Articles in Greenhaven Press anthologies are often edited for length to meet page requirements. In addition, original titles of these works are changed to clearly present the main thesis and to explicitly indicate the author's opinion. Every effort is made to ensure that Greenhaven Press accurately reflects the original intent of the authors. Every effort has been made to trace the owners of copyrighted material.

Cover Image copyright © Todd Davidson/Illustration Works/Corbis.

LIBRARY OF CONGRESS CATALOGING-IN-PUBLICATION DATA

Should junk food be sold in schools? / Norah Piehl, book editor.
p. cm. -- (At issue)
Includes bibliographical references and index.
ISBN 978-0-7377-5163-5 (hardcover) -- ISBN 978-0-7377-5164-2 (pbk.)
1. School children--Nutrition--United States. 2. Junk food--United States. I. Piehl, Norah.
LB3479.U6S56 2011
371.7'16--dc22

2010039238

Printed in the United States of America
1 2 3 4 5   15 14 13 12 11

ED028

Contents

Introduction

Pureed butternut squash soup, mushroom risotto, zucchini and red onion flan, organic black bean tortillas, pineapple gratin . . . Is this the menu for the latest trendy restaurant opening in town? No—it is a sampling of menu items offered as part of innovative school lunch programs around the country. For decades, public and private school children who bought hot school lunches as part of the U.S. Department of Agriculture's (USDA) National School Lunch Program became accustomed to chicken nuggets and corn dogs, perhaps with a snack cake or soda from the vending machines for dessert. Recently, however, thanks to growing public interest in food, cooking, and nutrition, children in some school districts are finding a lot more than pizza and macaroni and cheese on their lunch trays.

Part of the incentive for this renewed interest in the quality of school lunch is prompted by the revamped federal Child Nutrition Act (passed by the Senate and awaiting House approval as of September 2010), which mandates healthier ingredients; prohibits many high-sugar, high-fat items from being sold in vending machines on school property; and also provides the first increase in per-meal reimbursement rates since 1973. In addition, First Lady Michelle Obama's "Let's Move" anti-obesity campaign sponsors the "Chefs Move to Schools" initiative, a program that encourages working chefs to provide nutrition education and menu development for their local schools.

But doesn't this approach cost far more than old standbys like hamburgers and French fries? Not according to Jonas Falk and Justin Rolls, whose small company Organic Life, LLC, serves organic, free-range meals to kids in several Chicago-area schools. Founded in 2006, the company was profitable by 2009 and has even outbid major providers, such as Sodexho, in obtaining public school food service contracts. The key to the company's success, according to Rolls, is that these young entrepreneurs are bringing a new, scaled-down approach to school food service, an industry whose menu offerings and distribution channels have been stagnant for nearly fifty years. And, as one award-winning school food service director reminds others, the USDA's National School Lunch Program has always provided funding and support for schools to serve dozens of fruits and vegetables; it's just that old habits can be hard to break.

And what about the kids? Will they really eat unusual or unexpected foods like blueberry soup or sushi? Absolutely, says an administrator at one school where Organic Life serves lunch; there the number of students purchasing daily hot lunch rose to 330 from 225 during the course of the school year. One student at the school praised the change, saying "There are no more mystery meats."

Robert Surles (also known as Chef Bobo), the French Culinary Institute-trained executive chef at New York City's Calhoun School, argues that adults underestimate the sophistication of kids' palates. Particularly popular for its soups (including cauliflower, split pea, and miso), Chef Bobo's menus have resulted in kids eating a lot more vegetables—by request. Chef Bobo notes that when he first took over the kitchen, he was ordering just one crate of vegetables per day; now, "We've had to increase . . . to five cases, or we run out." Chef Bobo has managed to make all these changes without increasing the amount charged for school lunches or the number of staff members he oversees, although he does rely heavily on parent and student volunteers to help with preparing and serving lunches and promoting and modeling healthier eating to younger students.

Despite such examples of promising practices, schools still face major hurdles in efforts to retool school lunch programs to include innovative menus and healthy choices. Long-standing food service contracts, complex distribution networks, and established vendor agreements all mean that administrators and concerned parents must be dedicated, persistent, and patient if they want to bring about systemic change. Many U.S. schools no longer even have their own on-site kitchens (hot lunches are trucked in from centralized kitchens), further complicating chefs' goals of serving food that's both locally grown and prepared on-site, often with student or volunteer help. But, thanks to the federal government's renewed commitment to student health and nutrition as well as growing pressures from grass-roots organizations, the incentive for improvement is strong. Many schools have found the right formula of healthy food, great tastes, and budget-friendly prices, and their examples can serve as inspiration for parents, students, and schools eager for change.

1

Junk Food Should Not Be Banned in Schools

Margaret Johnson

Margaret Johnson teaches English and French at West Las Vegas High School in Las Vegas, New Mexico. She also has taught college English and worked in the Army Signal Corps in Germany.

Freedom of choice should be extended to students' school dining options. Providing plentiful choices—including the option to select foods that are less healthy—can keep schools from feeling institutional and can help enhance students' feelings of personal responsibility and satisfaction. Students who do not care for standard school menu options, or who cannot eat these meals because of dietary restrictions, often go without eating altogether. Providing attractive alternatives can help ensure that students maintain adequate caloric intake, which will in turn help enhance their attention and performance in class. In addition, sales of junk food can provide substantial economic benefits for schools.

Yes, junk food should be sold in schools—along with other food. Students will buy anything that costs under a dollar, is portable, flavorful, visually appealing, and gives them a quick pick-me-up. They like traditional candy bars, nutrition bars, pickles, lemons, sodas, fruit drinks, and water. I'm sure milk would be a top seller. Above all, students like freedom of choice.

Students often do not recognize cafeteria fare as food. The nutritionally correct meal in the garbage can has no nutritional value. Our politically correct cafeteria offers a wide variety of meals, all as well prepared as regulations and mass production allow. The bread is made on site.

But some students will not eat tomatoes, meats, spices, or other ingredients. Others cannot deal with the noise, long lines, and short lunch periods. Some don't have time to get seconds.

> *Our schools are restrictive enough as it is. They do not need to resemble prisons any more than they do already.*

Junk food provides quick energy, substitutes for missed meals, and supplements inadequate meals.

Medical and Economic Arguments

My learned colleague in biology says teens need munchies to keep them alert. I found this to be accurate when I grounded classes for not disposing of their trash properly. Without snacks, those who weren't antsy were asleep. Most were not focused.

I do not claim any medical expertise, but I am a teacher and a mother, and I have observed that caffeine is, for some, a better drug for hyperactivity than what is sold at the pharmacy, and a cola can help the student whose pharmaceutical wears off at noon. A school that bans colas and candy can cause a medical hardship. Also, denial, even for as short a time as a school day, can cause bingeing.

On the economic side, junk food can provide a steady income for school organizations at a better price and profit margin than the fund-raiser companies offer. Recycling cans is a profitable byproduct.

I do worry about where students get so much disposable income, but that is a matter for their parents to monitor.

Yes, we should teach and model good eating habits. Yes, we have health problems brought on by poor nutrition. But no, we should not ban junk food. Our schools are restrictive enough as it is. They do not need to resemble prisons any more than they do already.

2

Junk Food Should Be Banned in Schools

Will Dunham

Will Dunham is a staff writer for Reuters.

Current guidelines for foods sold alongside official school meals have been in place since the 1970s but they need to be updated. An Institute of Medicine expert panel recommends that lawmakers update guidelines to limit foods to specific whole grains, low-fat dairy, and fruit and vegetable options. In addition, schools should no longer sell sodas or other drinks with added sugar, and they also should prohibit the sale of caffeinated beverages. Abiding by these recommendations may help curb the rising rates of obesity and related health problems among schoolchildren. Because schoolchildren consume a high percentage of their daily caloric intake during the school day, they should have the highest-quality nutritional choices available to them at these times.

Sugary drinks, fatty chips and gooey snack cakes should be banned from U.S. schools in the face of rising childhood obesity fueled by those junk foods, an expert panel said on Wednesday in a report requested by Congress.

The Institute of Medicine panel proposed nutritional standards more restrictive than current government rules for foods and drinks sold outside regular meal programs in cafeterias, vending machines and school stores in elementary, middle and high schools.

They promote fruits, vegetables, whole grains and nonfat or low-fat dairy products and seek limits on calories, saturated fat, salt and sugar. The panel opposed caffeinated products due to possible harmful effects like headaches and moodiness.

The proposals would banish most potato and corn chips, candies, cheese curls, snack cakes such as Twinkies, "sports drinks" such as Gatorade, sugary sodas and iced teas and punches made with minimal fruit juice.

School campuses should be an overall healthy eating environment.

A 15-member panel headed by Dr. Virginia Stallings of Children's Hospital of Philadelphia crafted standards applying to items not part of federally sponsored meal programs, which already meet some nutrition guidelines. They do not restrict bagged lunches or snacks children bring to school.

"Because foods and beverages available on the school campus also make up a significant proportion of the daily calorie intake, they should contribute to a healthful diet. And school campuses should be an overall healthy eating environment," Stallings told reporters.

The Institute of Medicine provides advice on health issues to U.S. policymakers. These recommendations came at the request of Congress.

The American Beverage Association trade group said the industry already was changing the type of products available in schools to reduce calories and portion size, and had agreed to voluntary guidelines on items sold in schools.

Rising Obesity

Consumer advocates called the proposals vastly superior to existing Agriculture Department standards dating to the 1970s for foods sold alongside official school meals, and asked Congress to embrace them.

"They're recommending very strongly that schools no longer sell junk food and sugary drinks, and that none of the foods sold undermine children's diet and health. And that's really important these days because of the rising obesity rates," said Margo Wootan of the Center for Science in the Public Interest advocacy group.

Sen. Tom Harkin, an Iowa Democrat sponsoring a bill to toughen the existing government rules, said unenforceable voluntary guidelines by industry are not enough.

The panel proposed two categories of foods and beverages that can be sold in schools based on grade level.

One category should be allowed at all grade levels during school and after-school activities and should provide at least one serving of fruits, vegetables, whole grains, or nonfat or low-fat dairy.

Examples include whole fruits, raisins, carrot sticks, whole-grain cereals, some multi-grain tortilla chips, some granola bars, some nonfat yogurt, plain water, skim and 1 percent fat milk, soy drinks and 100 percent fruit and vegetable juices.

A second category should be available only to high school students after regular school hours, including baked potato chips, whole-wheat crackers, graham crackers, pretzels, caffeine-free diet soda and seltzer water.

3

Improving School Lunch Programs Is Complicated

Ed Bruske

Ed Bruske is a former reporter for the Washington Post. *He is now an "urban farmer" near Washington, D.C., where he also works as a personal chef, publishes essays on a variety of food topics, and writes the blog www.theslowcook.com.*

Current efforts to reform school lunches through public aware-ness and policy development face pragmatic challenges of imple-mentation and cost-effectiveness, as school districts try to shift away from policies and practices that are decades old. Even schools that are trying to follow new guidelines are hampered by lack of cooking facilities, unhealthy ingredients, and student re-sistance to more nutritious options such as fresh fruits and veg-etables. In some cases, so-called healthier options actually have significant amounts of hidden sugar. Bringing about systemic, rather than superficial, change faces significant economic hurdles. Under new governmental guidelines for improving the quality of school lunches, the increased cost of preparing food will far ex-ceed proposed increases in federal funding.

First lady Michelle Obama's new campaign against child-hood obesity, dubbed "Let's Move," puts improvements to school food at the top of the agenda. Some 31 million chil-dren participate in federal school meal programs, Obama noted in announcing her initiative last week, "and what we don't want is a situation where parents are taking all the right steps at home—and then their kids undo all that work with salty, fatty food in the school cafeteria," she explained. "So let's move to get healthier food into our nation's schools."

Last month I had a chance to see up close what all the school food fuss was about when I spent a week in the kitchen of my 10-year-old daughter's public school, H.D. Cooke Elementary, in Northwest [Washington] D.C. Chartwells, the company contracted by the city to provide meals to the District's schools, had switched in the fall from serving warm-up meals prepackaged in a factory to food it called "fresh cooked," and I couldn't wait to chronicle in my food blog how my daughter's school meals were being prepared from scratch.

It didn't take long for disappointment to set in. It started on the first day, as I watched the school's kitchen supervisor, Tiffany Whittington, prepare baked ziti.

First, she retrieved several five-pound bags of "beef crumbles," grayish-brown bits of extruded meat and soy protein, from a walk-in freezer and loaded them into a commercial steamer. Curly egg noodles from dry storage went into the steamer next. Then she mixed everything with a six-pound can of pale-looking spaghetti sauce containing "dextrose/and or high-fructose corn syrup, potato or corn starch," according to the label. As she stirred the concoction, she added preshredded mozzarella and cheddar cheese from five-pound bags. Whittington frequently adds cheese to the food for flavor, she said: "I think the kids really like it."

The eggs I saw being cooked the next day weren't much better. They also were flavored with cheddar cheese, but it looked more like cottage cheese. The scrambled eggs had been manufactured in a factory in Minnesota and shipped frozen to the District. Besides eggs, the dish contained many ingredients out of a food chemist's manual—modified cornstarch, xanthan gum, liquid pepper extract, citric acid, lipolyzed butter oil and medium chain triglycerides. A few minutes in the steamer, and it was ready to serve.

From what I observed . . . "fresh cooked" does not mean "from scratch" or even "fresh ingredients."

When she took office in 2007, the District's schools chancellor, Michelle Rhee, opted to privatize food operations. "The mayor and I want to introduce students to a variety of foods to help train their palates to choose healthier foods for the rest of their lives," Rhee said. The "fresh cooked" initiative was included in the city's contract with Chartwells.

"Fresh Cooked"

But from what I observed during my week in the kitchen at H.D. Cooke, "fresh cooked" does not mean "from scratch" or even "fresh ingredients." Most meals are made from processed foods that have been precooked and frozen. They're simply heated in the steamer or in a convection oven, since one of the things missing in the school's tricked-out kitchen is a stove. Meal components have been designed to require minimal time and skill to prepare. It's all part of an effort to squeeze school meals into tight local food budgets that hinge on federal subsidies.

Freshness and flavor are the first casualties. Fat is replaced with sugar as a go-to calorie booster. One of the most startling images from lunchtime at H.D. Cooke was the mad rush around the cooler where chocolate- and strawberry-flavored milk is stored. Sodas have not been served in D.C. public schools since 2006, but the dairy products served rival soft drinks for sugar content.

I found the amount of sugar in the flavored milk astonishing. An eight-ounce (one-cup) carton of chocolate milk from Cloverland Dairy boasts 26 grams of sugar—about six teaspoons—only slightly less, ounce-for-ounce, than Classic Coke

(27 grams). A similar serving of strawberry milk has more sugar still: 28 grams, putting it almost in the same league as Mountain Dew (31 grams).

In the breakfast line, strawberry-flavored Pop-Tarts were always on display. Along with a long list of additives, this 1.8-ounce processed pastry contains 16 grams of sugar, more than three teaspoons. Pepperidge Farm Giant Goldfish Grahams were another standard item. A 0.9-ounce serving contains six grams of sugar, or about 1 1/2 teaspoons.

Kids could also choose cereal. Kellogg's chocolate-flavored Mini-Wheats Little Bites contain six grams of sugar in a one-ounce serving, according to the package. Kellogg's Apple Jacks offer even more sugar: A 0.63-ounce serving delivers eight grams, or nearly two teaspoons.

Vegetables: A Hard Sell

Healthy-food advocates such as the first lady are convinced that more vegetables are key to breaking the cycle of starchy, sugary foods and obesity. "In my home, we weren't rich," Obama said as she recalled her youth during the "Let's Move" launch event last week. "The foods we ate weren't fancy. But there was always a vegetable on the plate. And we managed to lead a pretty healthy life."

Obama said she had lined up Chartwells and several other national players to embrace new standards that call for more fruits, vegetables and whole grains in school meals, as well as less salt and sugar. And the Healthy Schools Act pending before the D.C. Council calls for increased servings of vegetables—and not just potatoes.

But as every parent knows, serving vegetables is one thing; getting kids to eat them is quite another. A 1996 nationwide survey of school cafeteria managers by the General Accounting Office found that, in student meals, 42 percent of cooked vegetables—and 30 percent of raw vegetables and salad—ended up in the trash.

Meal items are designed at the factory to meet government nutrition standards but come out as barely palatable foods.

The vegetables at H.D. Cooke were hardly more appealing. I watched the kitchen workers prepare a 25-pound bag of frozen broccoli, cauliflower and carrots in the steamer. The vegetables were gleaming when they came out of the bag. But after being cooked, the broccoli was limp and drab, and after an hour on the steam table, it had completely disintegrated, clinging to the cauliflower and carrots in little bits. As students came through the food line, Mattie Hall, one of the servers, called out: "Do you want vegetables? Do you want vegetables?" And the kids replied: "No! No! No! No!" Hall, who is nearing retirement and remembers making school meals from scratch, said children will go to great lengths to avoid vegetables. Each morning she lines up 17 blue insulated bags on the serving counter and fills them with a snack of fruits or vegetables. Students arrive and carry the bags to their classrooms. They're supposed to return them at the end of the day. But Hall said some don't. They wait until the next morning, then show up at the last minute with their bags, knowing the vegetables have already been dispensed. Hall gives them bananas or apples instead.

When I asked my daughter about all this, she confirmed that where vegetables are concerned, the kids eat carrots, but not broccoli, zucchini or cucumbers. "They like to turn them into slush," she said. "They step on them in the plastic bag."

The Healthy Schools Act calls for serving minimally processed local produce "whenever possible," as well as using school gardens to teach children the benefits of fresh produce. In the past year, a D.C. Farm to School Network has formed to push the idea of making school food more appealing and healthful—as well as to boost local agriculture—by incorporating locally grown goods. Having worked with kids in school gardens myself, and as a food-appreciation teacher in a private elementary school, I know it works. Kids will gladly eat lots of healthful foods, including vegetables, given a chance to help in the preparation.

The scenes I witnessed at H.D. Cooke reflect a culmination of decades-long trends that have converged in school cafeterias—industrialized food methods, meager school budgets and government policies run amok.

A Monumental Task

To reduce costs, schools opt for unskilled workers who don't get enough hours to qualify for benefits. U.S. Department of Agriculture regulations permit schools to trade government donations of surplus farm goods for products full of chemical additives from giant processors. Meal items are designed at the factory to meet government nutrition standards but come out as barely palatable foods that do not occur in nature. Yet schools must induce children to eat the meals in order to qualify for the government subsidies they desperately need to keep their food operations afloat.

Federal payments—including $2.68 for each fully reimbursable lunch—total around $12 billion annually and feed roughly 30 million children every day, according to the USDA. That covers about half the cost of food service. Local governments pick up the rest.

For children in the 10 percent of D.C. households considered by the USDA to be "food insecure"—meaning they cannot afford a steady, healthful diet—school meals may be the best food they see all day. "Every day during the week, thousands of District children rely on public schools for their daily meals," said D.C. Council member Mary Cheh, author of the Healthy Schools bill. "The school system can't always control what children eat. But it is our responsibility to teach kids healthy habits and provide them with the most nutritious meals possible while they are in our care."

It's a laudable goal, and Michelle Obama's star power may help Washington and other cities reach it, but it's a super-size task. The Institute of Medicine, which authored the standards recommended by the first lady, says the new food requirements are certain to drive up the cost of school meals, even as school food advocates declare that President [Barack] Obama's proposed increase in funding for federal meal programs—$10 billion over 10 years—isn't enough to add even an apple to students' cafeteria trays.

A few days after my stint observing H.D. Cooke's kitchen, I returned to the cafeteria during breakfast time. Many of the kids were eating sugar-glazed cookies called Crunchmania Cinnamon Buns, along with chocolate- or strawberry-flavored milk and grape juice. By my calculation, this breakfast contained 13 teaspoons of sugar—and this in a city that the Centers for Disease Control and Prevention designated as having one of the highest levels of adolescent obesity in the nation.

For many food activists, schools hold out hope of a place where all children have a chance to eat fresh, wholesome food. But how do we get there from here?

4

Schools Should End Fast Food Partnerships

Anne Hart

Anne Hart writes a weekly column about parenting issues for the Savannah Morning News. *She also is the founder of the website* www.southernmamas.com.

Public schools are being urged to improve the nutritional quality of their offerings; their efforts, however, are continually undermined by fundraisers that partner schools with fast food restaurants. Many parents and school administrators are concerned that such fundraisers send kids the wrong message about healthy eating and also encourage children to develop a preference for unhealthy food. Although some fast food restaurants offer a small number of healthier alternatives, it would be far better to undertake fundraising activities that do not involve fast food vendors at all.

When you hear about budget-strapped elementary schools selling junk food to students or partnering with fast-food chains for "Spirit Night" fundraisers, you may assume that the fault lies with the Savannah-Chatham Board of Education.

You might complain to the school system's nutrition director, Althesia Maynard, or nutrition coordinators in her department. They're used to it.

But you'd be wrong.

Because those fast-food partnerships have the nutrition team just as upset as health-conscious parents, especially in the face of our local obesity problem.

Fast-food partnerships and school "snack" carts that sell junk food to kids are decisions made by individual schools and parent-teacher associations to supplement school budgets. The BOE nutritional staff has no say over whether an elementary school partners with Chick-fil-A to hawk chicken biscuits to raise money. Or whether an elementary school has a snack cart where kids can purchase sugar-laden treats.

The school system's nutrition coordinators have the difficult task of fitting school meals into caloric and fat-content guidelines while also making those meals appeal to kids. Yet, individual elementary schools can hold a Pizza Hut school spirit night fundraiser or sell snacks, no matter how high the fat and caloric content.

Maynard and the school system's nutrition coordinators question the message that fast-food partnerships send to kids when it comes to nutrition.

Elementary schools partnering with fast-food chains signals to kids that not only is it OK to eat fast food, but doing so is a way to show school spirit.

"We want schools to follow the guidelines, just as we do, to combat childhood obesity," Maynard said. "We'd also like to see schools find other means to raise money, rather than using fast food."

Parental Debate

Fast-food restaurants are pros at hooking kids early. You can't drive by a McDonald's without the kids begging to play at the eatery's playground, hug Ronald McDonald and have a Happy Meal.

Which is why having elementary schools endorse fast food to students is more alarming to some parents than middle or high schools doing so.

Elementary schools partnering with fast-food chains signals to kids that not only is it OK to eat fast food, but doing so is a way to show school spirit.

Emily Garcia's kindergartener's school has two fast-food fundraisers a month, usually Chick-fil-A or a pizza chain.

Garcia and other parents who don't frequent the drive-thru regularly believe elementary schools should exhibit a higher health standard. They don't want to introduce young children to food that has been linked with heart disease and diabetes.

Especially in light of the fact that in the Coastal Health District, which includes Chatham and seven nearby counties, 29.9 percent of people are obese compared with the state percentage of 27.1 percent.

"Fast food is so bad for little kids," said Garcia. "I can understand that they want to raise money for school and that requires picking something mainstream that a lot of people will purchase."

Suzanne Aultman, whose husband, Brian, is owner/operator of Chick-fil-A inside Oglethorpe Mall, says the restaurant offers plenty of healthy options for children to eat on their schools' spirit nights—grilled chicken, yogurt parfaits, fruit cups.

"If a parent doesn't want their child to purchase an occasional chicken biscuit, either don't provide the funds to do so or explain to your child that you don't want them to buy a biscuit."

Richmond Hill mom Susan Shami says schools should be able to partner with whomever they want in order to raise funds.

It is possible to raise cash without selling a single chicken nugget.

"It's up to the parents whether or not to participate," said Shami. "If enough parents boycott fast-food fundraisers, schools will stop using them to raise funds. On the other hand, if parents choose to participate, schools will continue using those partners."

Fast-Food-Free Schools

Not all public elementary schools use fast-food partnerships to raise funds. Charles Ellis Montessori Academy has an active PTA that undertakes all kinds of fundraising activities such as dances, movie nights and festivals. Other Ellis fundraisers include a pancake breakfast at Applebee's. Selling carnations, coupon books, DVDs of the school's opera and greeting cards of student artwork also raise money.

"There is no denying that partnering with a fast-food restaurant is a quick, efficient way of raising money for specific projects, and, depending on the need, we might consider that as well," said Charles Wooten, principal of Charles Ellis. "However, at this point, because of the active parent interest and enthusiasm for undertaking other projects and ways of going about raising money, we have not partaken in that as of yet."

St. Andrew's School, a private school on Wilmington Island, also found ways to raise money without relying on fast food.

Last year, the school had a successful "slow-food" dinner with local restaurants to raise money for an outdoor classroom that will be a place for gardening and ecology, proving that it is possible to raise cash without selling a single chicken nugget.

5

The Food Industry Is Not to Blame for Obesity

Pierce Hollingsworth

Pierce Hollingsworth is vice president for Custom Media at Stagnito Media, a publishing company specializing in the food and packaging industry. He also teaches courses at Northwestern University's journalism school.

Current efforts in the United States and United Kingdom to reduce the marketing and availability of junk foods go much too far, without addressing the underlying issues that cause childhood obesity and obesity-related illnesses. Making the food industry into villains over-simplifies a very complicated problem and deflects blame from parents and schools, who should be teaching children the values of physical activity and personal responsibility. Children actually watch fewer commercials now than they did thirty years ago; nevertheless, they have continued to become less active and fatter over that same period. Blaming the food marketing industry and commercials for obesity trends is a politically correct attempt at a "quick fix," which is unlikely to solve this substantial public health problem.

England: "A ban on confectionery, crisps and fizzy drinks being provided in schools looks certain to begin in September following the publication of advice to ministers by the new School Food Trust yesterday." (*Guardian Newspapers*, March 3, 2006).

Pierce Hollingsworth, "Food Cops on the Prowl," *New Products Magazine*, August 2006. Copyright © 2006 New Products Magazine/BNP Media. All rights reserved. Reproduced by permission.

United States: "Congress wants to expel all bad food from the nation's schools." (*Detroit News*, April 7, 2006)

Bad food or bad habits? Obesity is a well documented, nagging and very real public health problem—not just in the United States, but throughout most of the industrialized world. If we all ate from a limited menu, and if a few of those menu items were solely responsible for making us fat, then it would be easy to simply cut them from the menu or limit their availability. Or if certain foods were truly physically addictive and caused us to fatten up, much like cigarettes cause cancer, then banning them would be a no-brainer. But that's not the case.

The current rush to ban junk foods is a misguided—maybe even tragic—exercise in shallow political correctness and gross ineffectiveness. Efforts by the food industry, responsible public policy groups and trade associations to formulate more effective tactics appear to be too little, too late. Nevertheless, a coordinated long-term effort by the food industry is essential. There is no quick fix.

Schools have become the battleground. They're the current hub around which the blame battle revolves.

Make no mistake, food and the food industry are far easier to demonize, regulate and litigate than a culture of laziness and indulgence. It's less complicated to assert that kids are fat because they're victims of clever food marketing than to lay the blame on parents and schools not teaching personal responsibility and good habits, or requiring sufficient physical exercise.

A War in the Schools

This column has periodically addressed the rising tide of litigation and regulation slowly oozing into the marketplace—and warned that the trend will not only continue, but intensify. To that end, schools have become the battleground. They're the current hub around which the blame battle revolves.

In May [2006], the Federal Trade Commission [FTC] and the Department of Health and Human Services released a report recommending concrete steps that the food industry should take to change marketing "and other practices" to make progress against childhood obesity. The press release that accompanied the report was telling. It noted, in part: "[Report] participants acknowledged that many factors contribute to childhood obesity, but recognized that regardless of the causes, responsible marketing can play a positive role in improving children's diets and exercise behavior."

According to FTC Chairman Deborah Platt Majoras, "Responsible industry-generated action and effective self-regulation are critical to addressing the national problem of childhood obesity. The FTC plans to monitor industry efforts closely, and we expect to see real improvements."

She's not alone. Over the past several months, the food industry has been hammered by condemning studies and recommendations. Last December [2005], the Institute of Medicine [IOM] singled out food marketing as the leading cause of childhood obesity and called for government intervention. "If the industries' voluntary efforts fail to shift the emphasis of television advertising to healthier products aimed at children, then the [IOM] committee recommends that Congress pursue legislation . . ." stated Dr. Michael McGinnis, the report chair.

Our kids will just continue to get fatter—with or without junk food.

And most recently, in June [2006], a Washington, D.C., delegate to the U.S. House, (Dem.) Eleanor Holmes Norton, introduced a bill to restore the FTC's authority to regulate marketing to children under the age of 18, because junk food advertising is "urging our kids to eat themselves into bad health."

Television Is Not to Blame

The problem is that kids now spend more time on the Internet and listening to iPods than they do watching TV. In fact, studies show that the current kid generation is the first to truly multi-task—able to watch, type, communicate, play video games and listen to different media stimuli at the same time. This may not make them smarter or healthier, but they can do it.

No doubt marketing plays a role in influencing human behavior, particularly in a media-sopped culture. But the over emphasis on food advertising is a troubling waste of time. Kids are getting fatter, yet the FTC found that they see "significantly" fewer ads on television today than 28 years ago. As of last year, the average number of ads totaled 13 per day, versus 18 in 1977. A University of Chicago PhD candidate, Fernando Wilson, recently released data that shows kids' TV viewing actually in decline over that past 25 years—while inactivity has been on the rise.

Consider this:

If all but fresh fruits and vegetables were eliminated from school foodservice and television advertising, and if the government went one step further and placed quotas on calories and fat contained in fast food meals, would the childhood obesity epidemic be stemmed?

Of course not. Obesity is up in all age groups because of the low cost of food, wide 24/7 availability, sedentary lifestyles, and less stigma attached to being overweight. Yet food and the industry that manufactures and sells it are in the litigious/legislative cross-hairs. It's the politically expedient quick fix, unfortunately our kids will just continue to get fatter—with or without junk food. The food industry will do well to continue to support rational public policy and directly support efforts to promote exercise and healthy eating habits.

6

School Nutrition Campaign Is Pushing the Food Industry to Adapt

Marion Nestle

Marion Nestle teaches courses on nutrition, food studies, and public health at New York University. She is the author of Food Politics: How the Food Industry Influences Nutrition and Health, Safe Food: The Politics of Food Safety, *and* What to Eat: An Aisle-by-Aisle Guide to Savvy Food Choices and Good Eating.

First ladies usually champion some kind of social program. Michelle Obama's chosen cause has become an anti-obesity campaign aimed at children, families, schools, and the food industry. This is a key issue for the long-term public health of the country, and Mrs. Obama's efforts are praiseworthy. Although food manufacturers are paying lip service to the "Let's Move" campaign and promising to reformulate their products to make them healthier, their highly publicized efforts are probably still resulting in poorer choices than those offered by non-processed foods. We still have a long way to go before our food system is fixed, and making big changes will probably require even greater changes in public policy.

Skeptic that I usually am, I have nothing but applause for Michelle Obama's decision to adopt childhood obesity as the first lady's official cause. Lady Bird Johnson's legacy is the flowers that bloom throughout the nation's capital. Obama must want hers to be the flowering of better health for our nation's children.

Yes, Obama is sensitive to political realities. She calls her campaign "Let's Move" rather than "Let's Eat Less Junk Food." But its goals are crystal clear. Her campaign aims to improve food in schools and eliminate "food desert" areas without access to healthier foods.

The White House organic garden is an integral part of this effort. It is no accident that Will Allen, the charismatic head of Growing Power, the group that runs urban farms in Milwaukee and Chicago, spoke at the campaign news conference. Good food, he said, is about social justice. Every child should have access to good food.

This campaign reveals real leadership on a desperately important issue. Obama brings diverse groups to this table. She presses government agencies to take action. She exacts promises from Congress to make it easier for kids to eat low-cost meals in schools. She got her husband [President Barack Obama] to create a task force to tackle ways to prevent childhood obesity.

Reaching Out to Business

In addition, she is asking professional and business groups to do more to help kids eat better. I'm particularly impressed by her speech to the Grocery Manufacturers Association, which represents the makers of processed foods and beverages.

With masterful tact, Obama nonetheless insisted that the association "entirely rethink the products that you're offering, the information that you provide about these products, and how you market those products to our children." We parents, she said, want assurance that food companies will stop "teaching kids that it's good to have salty, sugary food and snacks every day."

Food and beverage companies are falling all over themselves—with much fanfare—to reformulate and to promise to restrict marketing that targets kids.

Yes, she avoids saying anything about soda taxes or other measures that might make it easier for kids and parents to make better food choices, but she is bringing childhood obesity to public attention in a fresh, new way.

Consider what her campaign is up against. Preventing obesity means eating less, often a lot less, of processed fast-food, snacks and sodas. This puts the makers of such foods in an impossible bind. Eating less is not good for business.

Short of going out of business, what can such companies do to help? They can reformulate their products to make them a little healthier. They can stop marketing their products directly to children. But this, too, is bad for business—unless it can be used for public relations.

Making Change

Indeed, food and beverage companies are falling all over themselves—with much fanfare—to reformulate and to promise to restrict marketing that targets kids.

PepsiCo, the maker of soft drinks and Frito-Lay snacks, says it will stop pushing sales of full-sugar soft drinks to primary and secondary schools worldwide by 2012. The new policy is voluntary, encourages rather than mandates, and assures school districts in the United States and abroad that the company will not tell them what to supply.

It keeps vending machines in schools and allows for continued sales of branded sugary drinks such as Gatorade, juice drinks, and sweetened milk.

Kraft Foods says it will reduce the sodium in its foods by 10 percent, also by 2012. This sounds good, but has a long way to go. Kraft's Macaroni & Cheese (the SpongeBob package) contains 580 mg sodium per serving and two servings per package. A 10 percent reduction takes 1,160 mg sodium down to 1,050 mg. Salt is 40 percent sodium, so this brings salt down to 2.6 grams—about half a day's upper limit for adults.

Still, these are steps in the right direction. Are they meaningful? You decide.

In the meantime, the Center for Responsive Politics, a nonprofit research group focused on the effect of money on public policy, says soda companies have increased by ten-fold the amount of money they spend on lobbying—no doubt to counter the threat of soda taxes.

What are we to make of these responses? They raise my favorite philosophical question: "Is a slightly better-for-you processed food necessarily a good choice?"

What would be better for preventing childhood obesity would be to make eating real foods the default. These, as defined by Oakland's Prevention Institute, are relatively unprocessed foods that contain nothing artificial. And they are produced in ways that are good for farmworkers, farm animals and the environment, and are available and affordable to all.

Getting to that point requires policy as well as voluntary actions. Perhaps I'm reading too much into Obama's campaign, but that's how I interpret it. I'm supporting it. How about you?

7

All Food Sales in Schools Should Offer Healthier Options

Tom Harkin

Tom Harkin is the junior U.S. senator from Iowa and a member of the Democratic Party. He was first elected to the Senate in 1984. While in the Senate, he has worked on issues related to disabilities, labor, and agriculture.

The U.S. Department of Agriculture (USDA) has broad oversight of the federally sponsored school breakfast and lunch programs. However, the USDA has little to no oversight of what is offered in vending machines, which are present in nearly half of public elementary schools and nearly 100 percent of high schools. Proposed legislation may help close that loophole and also offer additional options for fresh produce and beverage alternatives to soda. Legislative action, as well as financial incentives, may help promote healthy eating among school children by offering them a wider, more attractive variety of nutritionally sound food choices.

Kids today face a minefield of nutritional risks, yet with advertising and marketing of unhealthy foods at the saturation point, most are blissfully ignorant of the dangers. One survey found that scarcely any school-age children and adolescents meet all scientific recommendations for a sound diet.

It is no wonder the American Academy of Pediatrics calls obesity an unprecedented burden on children's health. Fifteen

Tom Harkin, "Rethinking School Vending Machines: Providing Healthier Alternatives at School," 2010, harkin.senate.gov.

percent of U.S. children and teenagers are overweight—triple the rate of 35 years ago, and a higher percentage than in any other industrialized country.

In recent years, our public schools have been inundated by candy, soft drinks and salty and high-fat snacks. We call this "junk food" for good reasons. These foods compete with and undercut federally supported school lunches and breakfasts, which are required to meet USDA [U.S. Department of Agriculture] standards for sound, balanced nutrition.

Schools are by no means the only place kids obtain unhealthy foods, but studies show they have become a major source. The U.S. General Accounting Office found that vending machines, snack bars or other foods compete with school lunches and breakfasts in 43 percent of elementary schools, 74 percent of middle schools and 98 percent of high schools.

The widespread peddling of unhealthy foods in schools is selling students short and undermining the best efforts of parents, educators, and school meals personnel.

Not surprisingly, vending machines and other sources of junk food have a clear negative impact on students' nutrition. A recent eye-opening study tracked a group of fourth-graders, who had only USDA-backed school lunches, into fifth grade, where they gained access to school vending machines, snack bars and other food sources. As fifth-graders, they consumed 33 percent less fruit, 42 percent less vegetables and 35 percent less milk than they did the previous year as fourth-graders. Plus, they ate 68 percent more fried vegetables and drank 62 percent more soft drinks and other sweetened beverages.

Closing a Loophole

The widespread peddling of unhealthy foods in schools is selling students short and undermining the best efforts of parents, educators, and school meals personnel. Remarkably, as a result of a decades-old court decision and Congressional inaction, the Secretary of Agriculture is virtually powerless to prevent vending machine and similar sales from canceling out the good nutrition in USDA-sponsored school lunches and breakfasts. It makes no sense that USDA sets standards for those meals but cannot do so for nearly all other food sales in schools, so I have introduced legislation to close that loophole.

Other solutions are already under way. One is an initiative I authored in the 2002 farm bill to supply free fresh fruits and vegetables to students—starting with just over 100 schools, 25 of them in Iowa. Students, teachers and administrators all attest to the tremendous success of this pilot program in fostering healthier eating habits. I am working to extend and expand it.

Schools in Iowa and across the country are acting to offer healthier options in vending machines, snack bars and other outlets. In Minneapolis, for example, North Community High School worked with its local Coca-Cola representative and actually increased the number of vending machines from four to 16. However, 13 were stocked with water or 100 percent fruit/vegetable juice, two with sports drinks, and only one with soft drinks.

Schools understandably worry that such changes will cost them needed revenue. Yet in the Minneapolis example, while soft drink sales are down, beverage sales more than doubled, and water became the new best seller—yielding a nearly $4,000 increase in annual vending profits. A number of other schools have also maintained or increased vending-machine revenue after offering healthier fare. And to encourage more schools to offer healthier choices, I favor modest federal financial incentives.

It is time for Congress to step in and improve the health of our students. Given the option, many students will choose healthy snacks over candy bars and potato chips. With thoughtful planning, the federal government, state governments and local school districts can work to replace junk foods with enjoyable, healthier alternatives.

It is not a question of whether we can afford to improve nutrition at school; it is a question of whether we can afford not to.

8

Government Regulation of School Lunches Goes Too Far

Jeannie DeAngelis

Jeannie DeAngelis is a frequent political commentator and columnist. She also blogs at www.jeannie-ology.com.

When the government starts to mandate what foods can and cannot be sold at schools, their reach goes too far. Frequently, the availability of attractive foods can provide a good motivation for students and can make school a more pleasant place to be. First Lady Michelle Obama and Secretary of Agriculture Tom Vilsack have promised to spend federal money to achieve their goal of healthier schools. Students, however, will not be as excited about the healthier, potentially less tasty options available in school vending machines.

One highlight for this first grade St. Robert Bellarmine Elementary School student was the Wednesday afternoon candy-drive. Once a week, Sister Marie Rose Christianson allowed disheveled kids in brown uniforms and crooked clip-on ties entry into our classroom to sell penny candy.

On the sly my grandmother would pass me a few cents from the linty pocket of her apron giving me access to a little bit of Catholic School candy heaven.

In fact, 40+ years later I can still remember the aroma of the thick strings of warm red licorice. Believe me, it smelled nothing like the institutional cafeteria wafting with the fetid odors of sweaty kids, bologna sandwiches, rotten fruit and warm milk.

Thinking back, I'm convinced hot cocoa and bagels ferried me through high school. Academically, I was less than mediocre. In fact I still wonder how I managed to graduate. The whole event is a blur save olfactory memories of warm peanut butter cookies and cheap pizza. Unhealthy school lunch choices and truant officers kept me coming back for more.

Agriculture Secretary Tom Vilsack plans to exorcise Oreos from vending machines and stock them with (gag) nutritious offerings like hermetically sealed organic carrots.

Being a kid in the 60's and 70's offered benefits students in 2010 lack. How depressing to learn, "the [Barack] Obama administration is expected to unveil a plan this week to bring healthier school lunches to children across the U.S."

If the government has its way, Sister Mary Rose Christianson might as well resign herself to cursive writing and knuckle smacking because the only "candy-drive" schools will be able to sponsor are "drives that ban candy and junk food from schools."

Representing the Feds, Agriculture Secretary Tom Vilsack plans to exorcise Oreos from vending machines and stock them with (gag) nutritious offerings like hermetically sealed organic carrots.

The First Lady [Michelle Obama] is "expected to be in the forefront of the program, having called for an end to child obesity." At a "healthy eating event" in Virginia, Mrs. Obama referred to [daughters] Sasha and Malia's questionable BMI [Body Mass Index]. A sensitive Michelle related to the audience, admitting even the Obamas, "Often simply don't realize that those kids are our kids, and our kids could be in danger of becoming obese. We always think that only happens to someone else's kid—and I was in that position."

Hey Michelle, could it have been the "Maxed Out Pepperoni, the packets of powdered Kool-Aid, the Ham & American Stackers, or the bite-size Snickers bars" fellow students spotted in Sasha's lunch box? But I digress.

According to Michelle's new [ain't it great to be a kid] policy all of America's children, including Sasha and Malia, will be treated to quite a different fare in their Jonas Brother lunch boxes. "The girls had to adhere to new ground rules—less burgers, low-fat milk, fruits and water instead of sugary drinks; the change was significant."

How will Big Brother accomplish the goal? "The administration reportedly asked for another $1 billion in addition to the $18 billion already set aside for the federal meals program in order to fund the initiative." The U.S. is not the first to nudge junk food-lovers toward better choices. In 2004, socialized medicine-blessed Britain received help from celebrity chef Jamie Oliver and $436 million dollars in healthy school lunch monies to launch a similar initiative.

In the near future, memories of cubed red dye #40 Jell-O, little brown bags of M&M's, French fries, and Corn Dog Mondays are slated to fade into the past. Michelle Obama, Tom Vilsack and the federal government plan to woo red licorice eaters to class with pumpkin rice laksa soup, government-provided Vitaminwater and a side of delicious soy chips. Yummy!

9

Budgets and Policies Make Changing School Lunch Nearly Impossible

Monica Eng

Monica Eng is a food writer for the Chicago Tribune.

Parents around the country are eager to get involved with improving the nutritional quality of their children's school lunches. The national school lunch program, however, almost seems designed to frustrate their efforts. Although small, locally inspired improvements are possible, larger changes are hampered by limited federal funding and by policies that allow menus to be guided, in large part, by children's taste preferences. If schools feed children high-fat, sugary foods, these types of foods will become what children will expect and demand, perpetuating a cycle that is very difficult for well meaning parents and school nutritionists to break.

On a frigid February day last year [2009], Michele Hays filed into Evanston Township High School with other concerned parents to talk with district administrators about school lunches.

One specific target of the parents' ire was a cafeteria meal called "Brunch for Lunch." As luck would have it, administrators brought a sample of the meal with them.

"When I actually saw it, it was so much worse than I thought it would be," she remembered.

"So I got up at the meeting and said, 'You may be meeting all the guidelines . . . but I think it is unconscionable that you are serving pancakes, a tub of maple-flavored high-fructose corn syrup and a side of cookies for lunch.'"

Too Big to Change?

Even for parents in relatively small suburban school districts, such as those in Evanston [Ill.], the school food system can seem too big to change. Despite Hays' unusually open access to administrators and legislators, her yearlong effort to cut back on the weekly "Brunch for Lunch" offering in Evanston's elementary schools has failed so far.

Children's preferences dictate the menu because if kids don't take the lunches, the food providers get less money.

But a *Tribune* examination of school food in Illinois' 10 largest districts found small positive changes are possible. Several districts serve only fruit for dessert four days of the week; some restrict nachos entrees to once a week; one has done away with breakfast Pop-Tarts; and some offer daily cold bars full of sliced fruits and vegetables.

Many of these changes have come at the prompting of health-conscious parents, the first generation to spend billions on natural and organic foods for their children. Hays recently persuaded Evanston-Skokie School District 65 to post pictures and nutrition labels for school meals online.

But substantial obstacles to change remain. Most parents, administrators and legislators agree that the national lunch program is underfunded, forcing providers to serve cheap, often low-quality, foods. The system is also structured to let children's preferences dictate the menu because if kids don't take the lunches, the food providers get less money. Those things probably won't change until Congress shapes the new rules for the Child Nutrition Act in the next few months [early 2010].

At the meeting Hays attended, school food service directors showed a slide show on the mechanics of the National School Lunch Program, which involves an array of government agencies, funding structures and rules. It left them feeling "like this is so much bigger and confusing than we could have imagined," Hays said.

Parents Are Getting Involved

Rep. Jan Schakowsky, D-Ill., recently visited her granddaughter's Evanston school to learn about the situation on the ground so she can help shape federal policy when Congress debates the nutrition act.

"It feels to me like there is a movement across the country with parents more concerned about school lunches," she said. "But it's not reflected on a federal policy level as far as I can see."

On her visit, Schakowsky participated in a passionate discussion that reflected concerns reaching beyond the Evanston schools.

One of the most contentious topics at the meeting, which Hays also attended, dealt with the most effective ways for parents to make their voices heard.

She asked what might happen if parents organized a boycott of objectionable meals and, for example, sent all their kids to school with a sack lunch on the day "Brunch for Lunch" was served.

After a long silence, nutrition services director Meghan Gibbons said a boycott would be financially damaging. Gibbons oversees the District 202 kitchen at Evanston Township High School, which also produces the meals for District 65's elementary schools.

The brunch lunch is the schools' most popular, and any sudden drop in sales would mean smaller reimbursements from the federal government. Gibbons suggested that parents discuss objectionable lunches with the food service provider.

"If there is something on the menu . . . that our parents don't like, we can look at it," said District 65 Superintendent Hardy Murphy, prompting Hays to note that she already has protested the brunch lunch for some time.

The mother of a third-grader, Hays said she packs a lunch most days but sends her son with lunch money when the district is serving "meals like bean burritos that we want to support."

Both Gibbons and District 65 food service director Christine Frole say they are frustrated with the paltry sum—roughly $1—they can spend on food for each lunch.

As Congress prepares to discuss the Child Nutrition Act, President Barack Obama has asked for an additional $1 billion in funding for school lunches, which would mean about 30 cents more per lunch. Other observers are lobbying for money to fund a $1 increase.

Many People to Please

Money aside, Hays thinks it's a mistake to let children wield so much power over the menu. District food directors won't even consider dishes that score lower than 80 percent approval ratings from student tasting panels.

Gibbons countered that she must please many different constituencies. "We have some parents who are particularly interested in reducing sugar. Some particularly interested in whole grains. Some who are particularly interested in reducing high-fructose corn syrup. Then we have federal and state requirements, so in order to appease all groups . . ."

"It's not just appeasing but rather following an empirical health standard," Schakowsky interjected. "Also I think kids can learn to like healthier things. Their preferences are not static. . . . One of the goals we have as a nation is to change and improve their eating habits."

Echoing the concerns of many health advocates and parents, Hays said: "I'm afraid that if we are not educating their palates now—rather than reinforcing their unhealthy preferences—we are educating them to make bad decisions."

When Hays suggested that hummus might offer a popular, inexpensive and protein-rich way to feed the students, Gibbons replied that many of the kids were not familiar with the chickpea dip, that tahini (sesame seed paste, an ingredient in the dish) costs too much, and the serving size would need to be very large to meet protein requirements set by the U.S. Department of Agriculture.

Still, hummus and fresh vegetables are served daily as a side dish at Naperville Central High School, showing it could be used as a healthful accompaniment to meals if not the students' entire protein serving.

Schakowsky acknowledged that changing kids' tastes "is a lot to ask of a school system. And [meals served today] sound much better than they used to be."

Major Obstacles

One of the central obstacles to serving healthy food is the fact that the system discourages experimentation. Any drop in lunch participation results in financial penalties for the caterer.

When it was suggested that the new lunch rules could reduce that risk—perhaps by guaranteeing a minimum reimbursement that could keep districts afloat while they try healthier options—Gibbons said, "I think that sounds wonderful. Now will Uncle Sam go for it?"

To that Schakowsky replied, "Well, I think getting kids to try new things is going to take some sort of creative strategy."

After the meeting, Hays said she was impressed with her tour of the King Lab Magnet School's lunchroom, which serves more fresh produce and less lunch brunch than the rest of the district. Still, she suspected that even this high-level meeting may have minimal impact on the juggernaut that is the National School Lunch Program.

"One thing that I think is important for parents to remember is that there are limits to how much school lunch can change," Hays said. "It will never be all organic; there will never be all fresh cooked foods. But hopefully we will get that extra dollar per lunch."

10

Limiting School Food Choices Can Go Too Far

Andrea King Collier

Andrea King Collier is a writer and W.K. Kellogg Foundation/ Institute for Agriculture and Trade Policy Food and Society Policy fellow. Her work appears regularly in national magazines, including Essence, More, Ladies Home Journal, Real Health, National Medical Association Magazine, *and* AARP Magazine.

New York's public schools are creating rules that will limit school bake sales, instead encouraging parent teacher associations and other fundraising groups to sell only fresh fruit and pre-packaged snack foods, including Pop-Tarts, Doritos, and baked potato chips. Homemade baked goods, however, will be off-limits except at very limited times. Parents concerned about this trend point out that homemade baked goods as a very occasional treat are far less nutritionally harmful than regular consumption of processed foods and sodas. In addition, teaching children to appreciate the effort and genuine ingredients that go into made-from-scratch baked goods could help give children a more discerning palate and respect for the process of cooking instead of enhancing their preference for readily available packaged foods.

Through a very sophisticated mathematical calculation, I have figured out that I have baked 1,532 cupcakes, cookies and little gooey pecan thingies for school bake sales. I hated every minute, but I did my tour of duty. And yes, I cheered when the last of my kids hit middle school and it became uncool for his mom to show up with cupcakes for any reason. But even I am horrified that bake sales are on the chopping block in the fight against childhood obesity. Bake sales? Really?

In New York, school officials are working to create a policy that would limit bake sales. In an effort to reduce childhood obesity, they are looking to ban baked good sales from schools, with the exception of one day per month or after 6 p.m. when very few people are around to buy or sell their wares. Instead, PTAs and other groups will be allowed to sell fresh fruits and vegetables along with some packaged items that are on the district's list of healthy snacks. Doritos are on the list. A chocolate chip cookie baked by Grandma, not so much.

I had a heated discussion about this issue with one of my young, zealous friends who is almost always a food buzz killer. "But don't you think that schools can raise just as much money if they sell carrots?" she asked. After a long pause, and much thought, I said "No, not ever."

Regulating Bake Sales

From a food policy standpoint, "Setting out guidelines for when and what is included in a bake sale may be a good way of modeling healthy food habits, which include variety and moderation," IATP [Institute for Agriculture and Trade Policy] Food and Society Policy Fellow Alethia Carr says, "A bake sale held monthly, is different from a weekly sale for fund raising. A monthly offering of baked goods, that are wholesome, good food, including those with fruits and vegetables in the recipe, demonstrates a form of good eating for our children, while infrequent enough to demonstrate moderation." Carr says, "We have to remember that in schools, we're really showing our children how to live. Let's make sure we're doing it in a way that promotes good health."

The focus [of bake sales] could lie more on education about moderation and less on dictating ingredients.

But are we going too far? Cheryl Danley, an academic specialist at CS Mott Group for Sustainable Food Systems at Michigan State University believes that it is a good move for schools to begin to control what is on the school campus and to look at the various ways children access empty calories. "There is something to be said for moderation and honoring and recognizing people's food cultures." She thinks it is important to have discussions and forums about such moves. "The New York City health department unilaterally ordered the transfat ban, and also the Mayor's food Czar created the 'green cart' program of fresh fruit vendors without consulting communities."

But is the little bake sale where moms and kids bring in homemade goodies the main thing that's making kids fat? Nancy Baggett, baker, writer and author of several books including *The All American Cookie Book*, says "the sugary colas and 'fake fruit' drinks that folks guzzle by the gallon and 1,000-calorie burger and fries meals they routinely chomp down are the real problem because they are on menus every day." She adds that, "home-made baked sale goodies are a special treat eaten only once in a while. We always had school/church/community bake sales as I was growing up and almost nobody was obese, and even a slightly overweight child was an absolute rarity." Baggett says, "The difference now is the fat-packed junk food and super-sized drinks, NOT the cupcakes from the PTA sale."

Maybe traditional bake sales can be teachable real world moments for parents and kids, where the focus could lie more on education about moderation and less on dictating ingredients. "It is important to teach children that they can enjoy an occasional treat as long as they engage in an appropriate amount of physical activity that allows them to burn calories and maintain a healthy weight," says Maya Rockeymoore, Ph.D., president of Global Policy Solutions. "School officials should consider acceptable alternatives to traditional bake sales such as 'healthy bite' sales that offer more nutritious food items or 'bake and shake' sales in which students purchase healthier baked goods while burning off excess calories with physical activity such as dancing, hoola hoop, or other active play options."

Homemade vs. Store-bought

"I think this knee-jerk reaction to the 'obesity epidemic' is wrong, wrong, wrong" says Jill O'Connor, baker and author of several books including *Sticky, Chewy, Messy, Gooey: Desserts for the Serious Sweet Tooth*. "I am no longer allowed to bring home-baked goodies to the schools and no cupcakes on birthdays either. But I can bring in processed snacks—as long as they have the nutritional breakdown listed on the package— are still permitted in limited amounts." She also comments that "as a country, Americans tend to swing from one extreme to another in an effort to solve such big (no pun intended) problems—there are no shades of grey, no middle ground."

O'Connor is a scratch baker and a food purist in her own right. She makes a firm distinction between baking cupcakes from a boxed mix and icing them with canned frosting and a home-baked chocolate chip cookie made from scratch. "Kids should be exposed to real, honest-to-goodness baking, so they know what GOOD is, and will be more likely to pass up a Twinkie or packaged cookie if they have sampled something better." O'Connor also emphasizes the larger, satisfying benefits of actually producing homemade treats. "Real baking takes time, talent, patience and skill. If you want something sweet badly enough and you go to the trouble to shop for the ingredients, and skillfully assemble them into a delicious dessert you deserve to have a taste."

I feel a bit like Scarlett O'Hara, disheveled, flour on my face, holding a cupcake up to the heavens, declaring "By God as my witness, I will never do a bake sale again!" But it won't be because I am going to singlehandedly make kids fat with lemon blueberry muffins, or because I personally feel responsible for increasing fiber intake in little children, or because I want to tear down just one more cherished tradition. It will be because I have baked my 1,532 cupcakes, and I am too lazy to do any more.

11

Most Packed Lunches Are as Unhealthy as School Lunches

Richard Garner

Richard Garner is the education editor for The Independent *newspaper.*

Only about 1 percent of children's lunches brought to school from home meet government-mandated nutritional standards in the United Kingdom. Parents frequently pack processed foods, sugary drinks, and snacks with added sugar. Almost no packed lunches include fresh vegetables, and few include fresh fruit or 100 percent fruit juice. Because a sizeable percentage of students eat lunches packed at home, parents need to be educated on better, more nutritious choices to include in their children's lunch boxes.

"You'll find they've all got chocolate and crisps [potato chips]," said headteacher Roy Tedscoe, ruefully, on hearing that *The Independent* wanted to inspect the content of his pupils' packed lunches.

He was not too wide of the mark—although children at his school did do markedly better than the national average, where only one in every 100 packed lunches meets government nutritional standards.

Chocolate abounded. The first lunchbox we uncovered at Coleraine Park Primary School in Tottenham, north London, contained a chocolate spread sandwich on white bread and a packet of crisps. Another included a cheese pastry, a packet of Hula Hoops and a chocolate biscuit. However, we did then unearth one containing an orange, orange juice, water and a chicken sandwich. Given that about 80 students at Coleraine Park come in every day with packed lunches, we were lucky to find one so nutritional in its content.

According to research published today by the *Journal of Epidemiology and Community Health*, just 1.1 per cent of children's packed lunches meets nutritional standards for school meals. A study of 1,300 lunchboxes taken to school by pupils aged eight and nine found that crisps, sweets and sugary drinks took precedence over fruit, vegetables and milk-based products. Permitted savoury or sweet foods with a low fat content, vegetables and permitted drinks including natural juices, milk and pure water were the least likely items to be provided by parents.

Inconsistent Standards

Only one in 10 children had a portion of any vegetable. More than one in four (27 per cent) had lunches containing sweets, savoury snacks and sugary drinks, while four in 10 had sweets and snacks but no sugary drink. Nutritional guidelines ban schools giving sweets, savoury snacks or artificially sweetened drinks for lunch but there are no rules for pack ups.

The researchers, from the Centre for Epidemiology and Biostatistics at Leeds University, said the evidence showed that food quality in packed lunches was "poor". "Most lunches contained restricted foods and drinks such as crisps and cakes," they added.

New standards for school lunches had brought "drastic improvements", they said. But with figures showing that about half of Britain's seven million pupils eat a packed lunch every day, the survey is bad news for the Government's drive to improve the quality of school dinners.

The School Food Trust, which promotes healthy eating, said the survey showed the take-up of school meals needed to be improved. "It highlights why buying a well-balanced school lunch is the most nutritious choice for children and young people," said its chief executive, Judy Hargadon.

She said the trust would support any school which adopted a healthy eating policy on packed lunches.

But, according to Mr Tedscoe, it is not as simple as that. Coleraine Park primary has issued healthy eating guidelines to parents of children who take packed lunches—but it seems that very few obey them.

"They argue that 'if I put broccoli spears in my child's packed lunch, they will not eat it and will throw it in the bin,'" Mr Tedscoe said. "The healthy food and the more unappetising food they aren't going to touch. The parents say 'I'll give them what I know they're going to eat'. To them, it's not about healthy eating."

What's in the Box? A Nutritionist Examines the Contents of Four Typical Packed Lunches

*No 1: Crisps, water, chocolate spread sandwich on white bread, cheese string.

*Verdict: "Nuts, dried fruit or dairy products such as yoghurt would be better options than crisps, as they provide more vitamins and minerals," says Claire French, of the School Food Trust. "This lunch doesn't contain any fruit or vegetables."

*No 2: Orange juice, orange, water, chicken sandwich.

*Verdict: "It's good to see fruit juice. Chicken is a low-fat source of protein but if you swapped it for ham or beef, the iron and zinc content of this lunch could be higher. Iron and zinc are important for intellectual development and a healthy immune system."

*No 3: Ham and cheese roll, banana, probiotic yoghurt drink, fruit juice.

*Verdict: "Both cheese and milk drinks are great sources of calcium, which is important for bone development. But flavoured milk and yoghurt drinks can contain high amounts of added sugars which harm teeth. This lunch does contain a portion of fruit but no vegetables."

*No 4: Crisps, chocolate biscuit, Turkish cheese pastry.

*Verdict: "Savoury snacks and confectionery products tend to be high in fat and sugar. This lunch doesn't contain either fruit or a portion of vegetables or salad. It is also missing a drink; including fruit juice would provide a portion of fruit as well as quenching thirst."

12

Removing Junk Food from Schools Has Many Consequences

Jessica Blanchard and Casey McNerthney

Jessica Blanchard is an education reporter and Casey McNerthney covers breaking news stories; both write for the Seattle Post-Intelligencer.

When the Seattle School Board voted to make a statement about student nutrition and cancel its vending contract with Coca-Cola, the decision prompted unintended consequences. Not only did students continue to obtain junk foods from nearby convenience stores, school finances suffered—the district lost more than $300,000 in vending contract revenue. Now schools are being forced to choose which school activities, events, and clubs to cut back, as they struggle to make ends meet without this surprisingly large portion of their overall budget. The school board is facing increasing resentment from individual schools, many of whom thought the school board was going to make up the budget shortfalls with other sources of funding. School administrators need to think carefully about all the ramifications of cancelling vending contracts, even if their intentions are good.

It was a lunch that would horrify a dietitian: a bag of Tropical Skittles, a Jones soda, two Little Debbie marshmallow treats, a deep-fried pizza stick and a bottle of sweetened iced tea.

The high-calorie, sugar-packed treats are standard fare for Cleveland High School freshman Tikisha Spires, who travels off campus for lunch each day.

The district had little luck persuading kids to change what they eat, but did manage to slash an important source of revenue.

It's certainly not what the Seattle School Board had in mind two years ago when it adopted a rigorous nutrition policy and canceled a lucrative vending contract with Coca-Cola. Chips and cookies were replaced in vending machines with granola bars and trail mix; sugary drinks are no longer sold in schools. Cleveland fell into line with other schools, offering healthier foods in its cafeteria and vending machines.

Teens such as Tikisha fell into line, too—out the door to find their junk food off campus.

"Our health teacher tells us about nutrition, but we sit in her class and eat what we want," Tikisha said.

The district had little luck persuading kids to change what they eat, but did manage to slash an important source of revenue that has forced some schools to cut student newspapers, cancel annual events and end other popular activities.

Here's why: The policy meant to discourage students from eating junk food has instead driven student business to the grocery stores and fast-food joints near the city's high schools.

That in turn led to a significant drop in revenue for middle and high schools, which in recent years have relied heavily on money from vending-machine sales to supplement their budgets for student-body activities.

District officials still are trying to determine the total financial impact, but say it's about $103,000 a year for the district's 10 comprehensive high schools—not including the $190,000 payment the district received and passed on to schools as a bonus for allowing Coca-Cola exclusive access to sell beverages to students.

In all, the district had received about $340,000 a year from the Coca-Cola contract, according to district documents.

At most schools, the money had paid for academic club events, school newspaper and yearbook production, school dances, transportation to athletic events and other activities.

Some high schools coped this year by raising fees for Associated Student Body cards or holding fundraisers. But not all schools can raise enough money, and some have pleaded with district officials to help make up some of the shortfall.

School Board member Michael DeBell, chairman of the board's finance committee, said he supports the nutrition policy but was troubled when representatives from several of the city's high schools reported they were hurting financially.

"They thought they might have to drop spring sports or cancel events," he said. "That's kind of when the red flag went up."

The School Board is considering pumping some money into the high schools to shore up their budgets this year, but it would be a one-time payout, district officials said. The amount has yet to be determined, though the district's acting Chief Financial Officer Linda Sebring said it would be less than $103,000.

It's unlikely the School Board would vote to change the nutrition policy, so district officials have been brainstorming other ways to raise money.

Ideas include having students come up with marketing plans for each school's cafeteria, or consolidating contracts for services such as yearbook production to one company to save money.

"There's sort of a crisis mode," said Dick Lee, a Ballard High alumnus who coordinates fundraisers as director of the district's Office of School Partnerships. "Schools saw this coming, some built up small reserves—but no one knew what the impact would be. . . . It's maybe been a little worse than expected."

For some schools, even those in more affluent areas, the loss hits hard. Ballard High School received more than $34,100 from the Coca-Cola contract and vending machine revenue in 2004. During the fall and winter of 2005–06, the new vending contract generated only $2,449—less than what the school received on vending revenue alone during September 2004.

To lower costs for athletic transportation, one of the school's biggest expenses, Beavers cross-country coach Bruce Drager obtained a commercial bus license and borrowed the district's only 32-passenger bus to transport athletic teams.

While many school and district officials say they support the goals behind the nutrition policy, they say it's frustrating to see hordes of students head off campus during lunchtime—taking their milk money with them.

"And still we haven't made a dent in it," vice principal Keven Wynkoop said. "As we come up with possible solutions, the costs continue to go up."

Ballard has cut the school newspaper budget, eliminated spirit buses to athletic competitions and ended Beaver Days—a spring celebration that included a barbecue, student-staff softball game and other outdoor activities.

"It's certainly not an integral academic portion of the school year, but it was fun," Wynkoop said. "It was a connection to school for people."

While many school and district officials say they support the goals behind the nutrition policy, they say it's frustrating to see hordes of students head off campus during lunchtime—taking their milk money with them.

Adding salt to the wound is what some view as the district's broken promise to come up with a plan to cover any costs schools couldn't recoup under the new vending contract.

At Rainier Beach High School, athletic director Dan Jurdy said lost vending revenue has meant the South Seattle school was unable to pay its cheerleading coach, homecoming activities were cut this fall, the student newspaper was eliminated and the school's yearbook is in serious jeopardy.

"We assumed we could pay the bills with money we thought we would receive from the district for the vending revenue we lost," he said.

Steve Nielsen, the district's finance director until late November, said promises that schools would get money from the district each year to make up for the lost revenue is an "urban legend."

"What we did say was we would help the schools figure out a way to make sure that no students would lose their ability to participate (in after-school activities)," he said. "We never said we'd use regular money and just backfill behind them."

District officials point out they've taken steps to help schools become more adept at fundraising, such as offering a series of workshops in the past year and a half. They've also contracted with Lee to come up with fundraising strategies for the high schools.

Lee already has organized several events and plans to hold a Breakfast of Champions later this winter in hopes of pulling in as much as $200,000. The district also has discussed the idea of instituting a student athletic fee—though nothing is planned for the next year.

But the idea of trying to squeeze more money from students or the community doesn't go over well at schools in poorer neighborhoods. At Rainier Beach, for example, about 60 percent of students are eligible for free or reduced lunch, indicating that South Seattle families have no extra money to give, Jurdy said.

That argument doesn't sway School Board member Brita Butler-Wall, who championed the nutrition policy.

She points out that the vending-machine money came from the pockets of students and school staff members—not the school district.

And there are plenty of healthy foods the schools could sell that would bring back student customers, such as smoothies or popcorn, she said.

If revenue is still not as robust as before, it might be time for the student body leaders to choose which activities are most important, and consider scaling back others, she said.

"It's sort of a good time for (them) to do a little soul-searching," she said.

Though the nutrition policy hasn't always been popular, it's important for the district to take a stand against childhood obesity and encourage students to adopt healthy eating habits, Butler-Wall said.

She recognizes that it's not possible to keep students from eating junk food, even at school—but that's never been the goal.

"It's not like a weapons ban," she said dryly. "If a kid wants to bring a can of Coke from home, they're certainly allowed to do that. . . . But it's a little different than saying, 'Our school officially promotes the drinking of soda pop as part of school spirit.'"

13

Schools Must Foster Exercise and Nutrition

Amy Klobuchar

Amy Klobuchar, the senior U.S. senator from Minnesota, was the first female elected to the Senate from that state. She serves on the Senate's Committee on Agriculture, Nutrition, and Forestry.

Good nutrition and physical activity go hand in hand. Although school nutrition programs are incredibly important, encouraging healthy levels of physical activity both during the school day and outside school also is an important goal. We need to provide children with greater access to physical education courses and recess, as well as walkable routes to school and readily available recreation facilities. Of course, nutritious food also is important, which is why the secretary of Agriculture should have oversight over all food sold on school grounds, not just the food served as part of the federal school lunch program.

As the mother of a 14-year-old, I've seen the inside of a school lunch room more than a few times, and I know firsthand that one of the biggest challenges parents face is making sure their children are eating right and staying active.

It's an uphill battle to help our kids learn to make good food decisions—particularly when they are too often presented with an a la carte lunch room choice of french fries or yogurt. Given this reality, it's no wonder that childhood obesity has grown dramatically in recent decades—more than doubling in the past 20 years.

According to the Centers for Disease Control and Prevention, one out of every three children in the United States between the age of 2 and 19 is overweight or at risk of becoming overweight. And nearly a quarter of all children between age 2 and 5 are either obese or overweight.

In addition to damaging our kids' health, obesity also hurts our economy. According to a *Pediatrics* medical journal study, the hospital cost of treating children for obesity-related conditions rose from $35 million during the years 1979 to 1981 to $127 million from 1997 to 1999.

People don't become obese overnight. Allowing our children to have treats in moderation—as in trick-or-treating—is one thing, but good nutrition involves discipline that must be learned and practiced on a daily basis.

Getting Schools Involved

So what can we do to get our kids to eat healthy foods? We need to first ensure kids have access to healthy foods. And schools play a critical role.

Currently, children consume 30 to 50 percent of their calories in school, making schools a make-or-break partner in the effort to improve the quality of our kids' diets.

By law, federally subsidized school meals are required to meet nutrition standards and comply with the Dietary Guidelines for Americans. However, food and beverages that aren't part of federal school meal programs are largely exempt from such requirements. This is especially concerning since only three out of 10 schools prohibit the sale of junk foods in school vending machines nationwide.

To address this issue, I sponsored the Child Nutrition Promotion and School Lunch Protection Act, which grants the Secretary of Agriculture the authority to regulate the sale of all foods and beverages on school grounds and requires national nutrition standards for these foods. Of course there will be an exemption for bake sales!

Two Halves of the Equation

Good nutrition is half of the equation. Exercise is the other half.

When I was a kid, school recess and physical education class were times for kids to run around and play games. These days, recess time is getting shorter and shorter and kids' waistlines are getting wider and wider.

The consequences of poor nutrition and a lack of exercise are serious. Obese children are more likely to develop Type 2 diabetes, heart disease and hypertension. Obesity also has an adverse impact on a child's academic and social performances. These consequences often last a lifetime since obese youth are statistically more likely to remain so through adulthood.

We also need to focus on prevention and provide kids with access to safe places to exercise and play. That starts in our neighborhoods. Studies show that people living in more walkable communities have a reduced risk of obesity, and children with easy access to recreational facilities are more active than those children with limited access.

Putting our children on the right path of good nutrition and exercise is a daily choice. It's not an easy task, but making changes in our schools and neighborhoods are essential steps to help improve the well-being of our kids and the long-term prosperity of our country.

14

School Diet and Exercise Programs May Go Too Far

Anne Marie Chaker

Anne Marie Chaker is a staff writer for The Wall Street Journal.

Diet and exercise are positive improvements, right? Maybe not, if mandated programs cause children and their families increased stress and embarrassment. New federal wellness policies have inspired some states to include students' body-mass index on their report cards or to encourage overweight students to enroll in special extracurricular exercise and wellness programs. Some parents and students complain that school districts' efforts have resulted in misclassification of students as overweight when they're just fit and muscular, and that school lunch efforts to cut back on portion size result in students being hungry at the end of the day. These new programs potentially harm children's self-esteem as well as the relationship between parents and school administrations.

Brittany Burns, 12 years old, has always been on the heavy side. Last year in fifth grade, neighborhood kids started picking on her at the bus stop, calling her "fatty" and "chubby wubby." Then someone else piled on: Brittany's school.

In a letter dated Oct. 2, 2006, the Campbell County School District No. 1 invited "select students" to take part in a fitness and nutrition program set up for some of the district's most overweight kids. At 5 feet 2 inches tall and 179 pounds, Brittany qualified.

Receiving the letter was "embarrassing," Brittany says. Her mother, Mindi Story, a clerk at an Albertsons supermarket, says she seethed "pure anger" because, she argues, her daughter's weight shouldn't be the school's concern: "I send her to school to learn math and reading."

A new federal rule requires that all school districts receiving meal subsidies create a "wellness policy" outlining goals for nutrition and fitness.

Spurred by a local doctor and an enthusiastic school board, Gillette [Wyoming] has banned soda and second helpings on hot meals. This year, it included students' body-mass index [BMI]—a number that measures weight adjusted for height—on report cards, and started recommending students like Brittany for after-school fitness programs. It even offers teachers the chance to earn bonuses based on their fitness.

While the extent of Gillette's weight campaign makes it an outlier, the school district is just one of many communities stepping up efforts to tackle childhood obesity. At the Buckeye Central Local School District in New Washington, Ohio, officials have replaced large cookies with smaller ones. Stewart Middle School in Norristown, Pa., has limited the number of snacks students can buy to one a day. Burning Tree Elementary School in Bethesda, Md., now asks parents to bring fruit and juice for class parties instead of chips and soda.

Arkansas, Pennsylvania and a few other states require that students' body-mass index be recorded and sent home to parents periodically. Starting this school year [2007], a new federal rule requires that all school districts receiving meal subsidies create a "wellness policy" outlining goals for nutrition and fitness.

Many health experts approve, given how much time children spend at school. Schools create "social norms," says Marlene Schwartz, Director of Research and School Programs at

Yale University's Rudd Center for Food Policy and Obesity. "The school is the perfect place to both teach things intellectually, but also create an environment where those lessons are reinforced."

A New Backlash

But across the country, the new rules are also sparking a backlash among parents, children and even some teachers and school officials. The efforts often draw derision for being too extreme and demonizing children. Arkansas, the first state to pass legislation requiring schools measure students body-mass index, backtracked last month and now allows parents to refuse the assessment. The question of weight in Arkansas has been a sensitive one since former Gov. Mike Huckabee shed more than 100 pounds a few years ago and encouraged locals to follow his example.

Everything the Healthy Schools Task Force has done has been controversial.

Rosey Barbour was a member of the Gillette "Task Force" that devised the health initiative. Her 12-year-old son Taylor, who attends Rawhide Elementary, was bullied for being overweight. Then in December, the family received a letter inviting him to take part in a fitness and nutrition program.

Seth Barbour, Taylor's father, "was a little past mad," he recalls, given Taylor's sensitivity about his weight. The Barbours never told their son about the invitation.

While on the task force, Mrs. Barbour fought some of its initiatives, in particular the move to put BMI scores on report cards. "Everything the Healthy Schools Task Force has done has been controversial," she says.

Gillette is a dusty, bustling coal-mining center in northeastern Wyoming, bisected by a railroad operated by Burlington Northern Santa Fe Corp., which delivers coal to such cities as Chicago and Centralia, Wash. Against empty sky, a water tower proclaims the city the "Energy Capital of the Nation."

Fueled by that thriving industry, the town's population is booming. In the past five years, its population has risen steadily, by about 20% to 27,533. Tax revenue from local mines helps fund recreational activities for young, sports-minded families, including an Olympic-size swimming pool and a nine-hole golf course.

Wyoming redistributes local property-tax revenue state-wide to ensure that poorer districts aren't left out. Campbell County is so wealthy, however, that its school district in recent years has received a "recapture rebate" after remitting funds to the state. The school district tapped that money to fund some of the health programs, to the tune of $500,000 a year. The rest—$250,000—comes from the Campbell County Community Public Recreation District, which levies property taxes on energy companies.

About three years ago, for the first time in his nearly 20 years as a doctor in the area, school board chairman and local pediatrician David Fall started seeing cases of overweight children with diabetes. An informal survey of patients suggested that about 15% were overweight, close to the national average. Those who were overweight, he noticed, were "way overweight." At the school board, he says, "we decided this was an issue we should look into."

Across the U.S., about 17% of children and adolescents age two to 19 are overweight, more than triple the percentage of 30 years ago, according to the federal Centers for Disease Control and Prevention [CDC]. The CDC defines overweight children as those with a body-mass index in the 95th percentile and above, which puts them at increased risk for chronic health problems such as hypertension, certain types of diabetes and heart disease.

Healthy Schools Task Force

In 2004, Dr. Fall organized the Healthy Schools Task Force and recruited about two dozen parents and teachers. First item on the list: Removing soda machines from schools in the district. "The biggest grief we got was from the teachers," Dr. Fall recalls, because schools also took machines out of teachers' lounges. "Some of them are still mad at me. They called me the 'Pop Nazi.'"

The task force decided students would no longer receive second helpings of lunch entrees (they could have unlimited helpings of fresh fruits, vegetables and salad). It told lunch servers to give smaller portions to younger students. Concession-stand vendors received a list of recommended alternatives, such as fresh fruit and string cheese. School principals were pushed to dump bake sales in favor of car washes, talent shows and walkathons.

The task force also deployed financial incentives. Elementary schools that added physical activity received extra funding for instructors and after-school health programs. Based on the assumption that children emulate adults around them, the district in February began awarding bonuses to faculty who opted to receive a fitness assessment, which measured metrics such as blood pressure and bicep strength. The better the fitness score, the higher the bonus—as much as $160 if they take the test twice a year and get high marks.

Toward the end of 2004, parents started complaining at task-force meetings that their children were coming home hungry. One parent criticized the group for making unilateral decisions without involving the community.

"My kids are in every sport there is," says parent Mary Lou Gladson, who attended one of the meetings. "But they aren't big fruit and vegetable eaters. My kids were getting the short end of the stick because of the obese kids."

Even determining who is overweight has proven nettlesome. Nine-year old Jeremy Holwell, who attends Lakeview

Elementary, swims in a local league several nights a week and plays baseball in the summer. Gesturing to his Spiderman-theme room littered with dozens of swimming ribbons and pentathlon trophies, his mother Stephanie says: "I mean, this kid's active."

In January, Mrs. Holwell noticed a fitness assessment at the bottom of his nearly straight-A report card. Jeremy placed in the 97th national percentile: "overweight," according to the report. She asked the principal to stop including the information on Jeremy's report card, which he agreed to do.

[According to Dr. Fall] the importance of the program "outweighs any temporary hurt feelings."

Sue Harter, the district's director of food service, says the strictures are becoming overly specific. Snacks sold during the school day can contain no more than seven grams of fat, no more than two grams of saturated fat, and no more than 15 grams of sugar, with a few exceptions. That means no french fries, Tater Tots or Twinkies. Ms. Harter was fine with that, but has balked at a proposal to take away other offerings, including beef jerky and baked chips. "I feel that kids junior high and up should be able to make choices," she says.

Talking about the district's campaign is hard for Ms. Harter. "I was a chunky kid. I've always struggled with my weight," she says, tears welling up. "Here I am, the director of food service, and I'm overweight." Because of the new focus on faculty health, "it gives you a feeling of insecurity," she says.

Dr. Fall says that beyond a few negative comments, he doesn't think there has been much public opposition. In any case, the importance of the program "outweighs any temporary hurt feelings," he says. "The kids know they're overweight! They don't want to be overweight! They don't want to be unhappy."

Troubling Letter

This school year, Dr. Fall intensified his efforts. By December 2006, 171 parents of children in grades three through six had received a letter offering a children's health evaluation and a related fitness program.

Mike Miller, a physical-education [PE] teacher hired to run the Healthy Schools initiatives, asked PE teachers to recommend students who might benefit from the program, which would be held after school.

Jim Coca, a physical-education instructor at Wagonwheel Elementary, says he reluctantly gave about 20 names to Mr. Miller, based on the kids with the lowest fitness scores. "I would have rather seen all the kids get a letter," he says. "Make it available to everyone, and you've hurt nobody."

A fifth-grade girl approached Mr. Coca after noticing the letter, addressed to her parents, on the kitchen table. "Mr. Coca, do you think I'm fat?" he recalls her asking. "I knew it hurt our relationship a little bit. She had never thought that she was heavy." Next year, Mr. Coca says, he won't give names. He'll send the fitness data to Mr. Miller and ask him to pick.

Mr. Miller says the PE teachers "would be the better ones to assess kids," but he says he'll use the raw data if necessary. "It will be obvious to us from the BMI and fitness scores if the kid's at risk."

Of nearly 200 letters that went out to families, only 23 parents made an appointment. They were invited to a "Strong Kids Club" exercise group that meets after school at a local recreation center three times a week.

Erin Wiley, the assessment program's coordinator, is an enthusiastic, ponytailed 24-year-old who leads third to sixth graders in an hour of exercises. On a recent Tuesday, after teaching eight kids a leg exercise using resistance cords, she wound down the session with a series of yoga poses named after animals—cobra, swan, downward dog, cat and cow.

"How much more of these are we going to do?" whined seven-year-old Ryan Quintana, a second-grader from Pronghorn Elementary School who suffers from asthma.

"It's a whole series!" said Ms. Wiley. "Want to see 'volcano'?"

Many of the families say the assessments and classes—which are free—have helped their kids.

Ryan, for example, was always bigger than his peers in his class, but seemed unaware of it until recently. "I noticed him saying, 'This shirt makes my belly look big' while getting dressed," says his mother, Jaime. "We realized he needs to lose weight."

He has been attending classes three times a week since the fall. He used to dread gym. Now, says his father, Robert, "he talks about how fast he was. I don't think he's Flash Gordon by any means, but he's come a long way."

By the time of his follow-up assessment, Ryan had grown an inch, to 4 feet 6 inches, and had lost two pounds, to 104. He went from a high "body composition," a measure of body fat, to average. His fitness level rose from "fair" to "average."

Before, PE class was "too hard for me," Ryan says. "I had to take my inhaler." Now, he says, it is "not so scary."

Giving the Program a Chance

Faith Rudland is a 10-year-old fifth-grader at Conestoga Elementary who also attends the fitness classes. When her mother, Heather, received the invitation letter, she was relieved to be getting some help.

"It's not like I'm blind," Mrs. Rudland says. The family had sought the advice of doctors and dieticians to bring down Faith's weight, but nothing worked. One said to watch sodium intake. Another said she would grow into her weight.

When Faith started the Strong Kids Club, she weighed 163 pounds. Now she weighs 145. "It's a learning process for me, too," says Mrs. Rudland, who has cut back on Hamburger Helper and now stocks the fridge with fruit and vegetables.

Faith says the classes "make my life a lot better." She now doesn't get as winded when she runs and earns higher marks in PE.

For other families, the program is an unwelcome intrusion. Brittany Burns "has been a big kid since she was little," says Mrs. Story, her mother. "We're a big-boned family, as is a lot of Wyoming. It's a meat and potatoes state," she says.

Later, she prepares a dinner of exactly that when her husband and brother-in-law come home from the mines, their faces and hands black with grime.

Mrs. Story says that when the letter came, she decided to give the program a chance. She took her daughter, who attends Lakeview Elementary, to an assessment. Brittany started writing down what she ate. By the end of the week, her enthusiasm flagged. She never went back for a follow-up.

"I didn't push the issue," says Mrs. Story. "I didn't want her to think I saw her the same way these people saw her."

15

Planting School Gardens Can Change Kids' Eating Habits

Pearl Tesler

Pearl Tesler is a science writer at San Francisco's Exploratorium museum.

It is difficult to sell healthy food options to children with promises of increased nutrient intake and improved fiber content. But if schools can teach kids that growing and preparing healthy food can be a fun social activity—and that it can taste good, too—they have a real opportunity to change behavior and eating habits for the better. That is the principle behind the Edible Schoolyard program, which started in the mid-1990s in California and spread to many schools across the country. Students grow and harvest their own food, prepare healthful meals based on the fresh fruits and vegetables they have grown, and then enjoy a leisurely meal together. This program allows students to excel at tasks outside traditional academic disciplines and also to gain appreciation for real, unprocessed foods.

"What's for lunch?" For many kids, the answer is either mystery meat and fries from the school cafeteria or chips and a soft drink from the vending machine. But for students at Martin Luther King Jr. Middle School in Berkeley, California, the answer might be red-bean stew, stuffed grape leaves, or potato-and-chive biscuits. Not only do the students eat these gourmet meals, they cook them—and even grow the ingredients right on the school grounds, in an organic garden

Pearl Tesler, "The Lunch Bunch," *Current Health 2*, March 2005. Copyright © 2005 Weekly Reader Publishing. All rights reserved. Reproduced by permission.

that they plant and tend themselves. In organic gardens, natural products—not chemicals—are used to control pests and weeds and to help crops grow.

The program, known as the Edible Schoolyard, was started in 1994 by the famous chef Alice Waters. Her goals: to raise student awareness of where food comes from and to promote more healthful eating habits. Waters is an advocate of slow food—food that takes more time to prepare than fast food but that is also better-tasting and better for you.

Garden-Variety Goods

An island of green in urban Berkeley, the Edible Schoolyard garden sits on a 1-acre plot that used to be a parking lot. The thriving garden boasts traditional fruits and vegetables, such as raspberries, tomatoes, artichokes, and peas, along with more exotic fare, such as kiwifruit, tomatillos, and bok choy. Nearby, in the fully equipped kitchen, students turn harvested garden crops into dishes fit for a king or queen.

"What we're hoping to do is introduce students to where food comes from and to empower them to make conscious food choices that affect their health," program coordinator Chelsea Chapman told *Current Health* [CH]. "Kids are so inundated with advertising, peer pressure, and everything they see on TV—stuff like blue macaroni and cheese. You can't just expect them to go in and happily eat chard and kale and broccoli unless they have some kind of positive exposure to it."

Lending a Hand

When it's time to divvy up chores in the Edible Schoolyard garden, students volunteer for the tasks they prefer. On the day that CH visited, the options included turning compost (a mixture of decaying vegetation and manure used as a fertilizer), cultivating garden beds, and harvesting crops.

The compost crew uses pitchforks to stir up the foul-smelling mass that will ultimately be spread in the garden. "Ewww, it stinks!" howled one shoveler. "Not as bad as my brother," joked another.

Meanwhile, in another part of the garden, the harvesting crew is collecting green beans, red Swiss chard, and potatoes. They carry the vegetables directly to the kitchen for today's recipe—frittata, a vegetable pie made with eggs. The eggs come courtesy of the chickens that live in a coop in one corner of the garden.

Later on, in the kitchen, the students have 90 minutes to prepare and eat their homegrown feast. The kids quickly wash up, tie on aprons, and start breaking eggs and chopping vegetables. "I've never made this before," said eighth grader Alonzo Cudjo. He expertly sautes the chopped vegetables for his group's frittata, even though, he admitted to CH, he doesn't get to cook at home. "I'm not allowed to touch the stove after that pancake incident in the fourth grade."

The chance to discover unknown skills is one of the many benefits of the Edible Schoolyard program, said assistant program coordinator Natsumi Iimura. "The kids who aren't the smart kids in the classroom have an opportunity to shine. Someone who's booksmart might be completely clueless in the garden or kitchen. It's kind of an equalizer."

Naturally, there have been mishaps. Every so often someone confuses the salt and the sugar, with disastrous-tasting results. Once, a poorly flipped pancake landed on a stove burner, resulting in a fire alarm that had the entire school waiting outside for 20 minutes. But today everything goes smoothly.

Unforgettable Edibles

While the frittatas bake in the oven, students unfold red-checkered tablecloths and set the table. Part of the Edible Schoolyard tradition is to sit down together to share a meal and catch up on the morning's events. As the frittatas are finally served—and eagerly consumed—lively discussions fill the air.

Eight grader Tiara Swearington says she values the social aspect of the experience as much as the other parts. "All day at school we learn theories and stuff, but here, everyone just gets to relax and chill out. We cook and eat and talk and get to know each other," she told CH. "If it wasn't for this, I wouldn't know half the people in my class."

Others, such as Serene Walsh, find themselves eating differently as a result of their time in the Edible Schoolyard. What has changed? "I eat more fruits and vegetables," said Serene.

A Healthy Habit

More fruits and vegetables are exactly what teenagers need, says Mary McKenna, a nutritionist at the Centers for Disease Control and Prevention in Atlanta. According to McKenna, teens in the United States are increasingly aware of the connection between eating habits and health. However, they haven't fully mended their junk-food-eating ways. Teens still eat "too much fat, too much saturated fat, too few fruits, too few vegetables, not enough fiber, and not enough calcium," she said.

Changing bad eating habits isn't easy, acknowledges McKenna. "The environments in which we make food choices play a big role. If kids are going to eat [more healthful] foods and beverages, we have to make them available," she said.

More than that, the foods have to taste good. "To say, 'Eat broccoli because it has beta-carotene and phytochemicals in it,' well, I don't think that makes broccoli sound all that attractive," McKenna said. "I'd like to see people enjoy the taste of [healthful] eating, because the things that we enjoy, we tend to repeat."

Food for Thought

Today, frittatas. Tomorrow, who knows? The Edible School-yard is teaching kids—one home-cooked meal at a time—that nutrition isn't just about healthful food. It's also a matter of good taste.

16

Planting School Gardens Is a Misuse of Academic Resources

Caitlin Flanagan

Caitlin Flanagan is a writer and social critic who often writes about the conflicts and contradictions in present-day life, especially for contemporary women. She is a frequent contributor to The Atlantic.

The Edible Schoolyard program has taken off in schools nationwide, but especially in California, where the public schools are in crisis. Not only do these programs seem patronizing toward minority children, they also rob the most vulnerable students of far more valuable dedicated attention to traditional academic subjects. If we hope to help at-risk populations begin to eat more healthfully, governments should be focusing on improving overall social status and financial security, not on imposing irrelevant agendas on an already over-scheduled school day.

Imagine that as a young and desperately poor Mexican man, you had made the dangerous and illegal journey to California to work in the fields with other migrants. There, you performed stoop labor, picking lettuce and bell peppers and table grapes; what made such an existence bearable was the dream of a better life. You met a woman and had a child with her, and because that child was born in the U.S., he was made a citizen of this great country. He will lead a life entirely different from yours; he will be educated. Now that child is about to begin middle school in the American city whose name is synonymous with higher learning, as it is the home of one of the greatest universities in the world: Berkeley. On the first day of sixth grade, the boy walks though the imposing double doors of his new school, stows his backpack, and then heads out to the field, where he stoops under a hot sun and begins to pick lettuce.

It's rare for an immigrant experience to go the whole 360 in a single generation—one imagines the novel of assimilation, *The White Man Calls It Romaine.* The cruel trick has been pulled on this benighted child by an agglomeration of foodies and educational reformers who are propelled by a vacuous if well-meaning ideology that is responsible for robbing an increasing number of American schoolchildren of hours they might otherwise have spent reading important books or learning higher math (attaining the cultural achievements, in other words, that have lifted uncounted generations of human beings out of the desperate daily scrabble to wrest sustenance from dirt). The galvanizing force behind this ideology is Alice Waters, the dowager queen of the grown-locally movement. Her goal is that children might become "eco-gastronomes" and discover "how food grows"—a lesson, if ever there was one, that our farm worker's son might have learned at his father's knee—leaving the [writings of Ralph Waldo] Emerson and [Thomas] Euclid to the professionals over at the schoolhouse. Waters's enormous celebrity, combined with her decision in the 1990s to expand her horizons into the field of public-school education, has helped thrust thousands of schoolchildren into the grip of a giant experiment, one that is predicated on a set of assumptions that are largely unproved, even unexamined. That no one is calling foul on this is only one manifestation of the way the new Food Hysteria has come to dominate and diminish our shared cultural life, and to make an educational reformer out of someone whose brilliant cookery and laudable goals may not be the best qualifications for designing academic curricula for the public schools.

Alice Waters

Waters, described by her biographer, Thomas McNamee, as "arguably the most famous restaurateur in the United States," is, of course, the founder of Chez Panisse, in Berkeley, an eatery where the right-on, "yes we can," ACORN [Association of Community Organizations for Reform Now]-loving, public-option-supporting man or woman of the people can tuck into a nice table d'hôte menu of scallops, guinea hen, and tarte tatin for a modest 95 clams—wine, tax, and oppressively sanctimonious and relentlessly conversation-busting service not included. (I've had major surgeries in which I was less scrupulously informed about what was about to happen to me, what was happening to me, and what had just happened to me than I've been during a dinner there.) It was at Chez Panisse that Waters worked out her new American gastronomic credo, which is built on the concept of using ingredients that are "fresh, local, seasonal, and where possible organic." Fair enough, and perfectly delicious, but the scope of her operation—which is fueled not only by the skill of its founder, but also by the weird, almost erotic power she wields over a certain kind of educated, professional-class, middle-aged woman (the same kind of woman who tends to light, midway through life's journey, on school voluntarism as a locus of her fathomless energies)—has widened so far beyond the simple cooking and serving of food that it can hardly be quantified. As McNamee rightly observes, Chez Panisse

> is a much larger enterprise than a restaurant. It is a standard-bearer for a system of moral values. It is the leader of a style of cooking, of a social movement, and of a comprehensive philosophy of doing good and living well.

This notion—that it is agreeably possible to do good (school gardens!) and live well (guinea hens!)—bears the hallmark of contemporary progressivism, a kind of win-win, "let them eat tarte tatin" approach to the world and one's place in it that is prompting an improbable alliance of school reformers, volunteers, movie stars, politicians' wives, and agricultural concerns (the California Fertilizer Foundation is a big friend of school gardens) to insert its values into the schools.

Edible Schoolyards

The Edible Schoolyard program was born when Waters noticed a barren lot next to the Martin Luther King Jr. Middle School in Berkeley. Inspired by the notion that a garden would afford students "experience-based learning that illustrates the pleasure of meaningful work, personal responsibility, the need for nutritious, sustainably raised, and sensually stimulating food, and the important socializing effect of the ritual of the table," and spurred on by the school principal, Waters offered to build a garden and help create a curriculum to go along with it.

Fads in education tend to take off quickly, but nothing else has come into our public schools at the rocket-blast rate of school gardens.

An Aztec dance troupe performed on the day the first cover crop was planted (imagine it as a set piece for *The White Man Calls It Romaine*), and soon the exciting garden had made its influence felt across the disciplines. In English class students composed recipes, in math they measured the garden beds, and in history they ground corn as a way of studying pre-Columbian civilizations. Students' grades quickly improved at King, which makes sense given that a recipe is much easier to write than a coherent paragraph on *The Crucible*.

Fads in education tend to take off quickly, but nothing else has come into our public schools at the rocket-blast rate of school gardens, particularly here in my home state of California. To be sure, this was hardly a new phenomenon in California, where school gardens waxed and waned over the years, propelled by the state's agricultural interests, the back-to-the-land movement of the '70s, and so on.

But by the time Waters came onto the scene, organic food, nutrition, and sustainability were becoming the pet issues of the volunteering set. In the 1990s, Waters found a powerful ally in Delaine Eastin, the newly elected state superintendent of instruction (herself a "devoted gardener, home cook and recycler"), who called for "A Garden in Every School" the same year the Edible Schoolyard began.

Together, the bureaucrat and the celebrity paved the way for an enormous movement: by 2002, 2,000 of the state's 9,000 schools had a garden, and by 2008 that number had risen to 3,849, and it continues to grow. Waters, with her charisma and high political profile (which includes her friendship with the [President Bill and Secretary of State Hillary] Clintons), has been hailed as one of the most important educational innovators not just in the state, but in the nation. In 1998, she received an Excellence in Education Award from Senator Barbara Boxer, as well as an Education Heroes Award from the U.S. Department of Education; the Smithsonian has sponsored an Edible Schoolyard exhibit on the National Mall in Washington, D.C. Only four school gardens across the country bear the coveted Chez Panisse Foundation imprimatur (just two of them in California), but their influence has been profound. Not only has the foundation published a mind-numbingly earnest series of books on lesson planning, policy planning, and public policy, but it also has a teacher-training program and offers regular tours of the garden at King. In July [2009], a *Los Angeles Times* article was titled "A New Crop of School Gardens: Even as State Funds Are Wilting, Support for School Gardens Is Still Growing." Maria Shriver, the first lady of California, is a strong supporter and, like all the proponents of this kind of education, she urges schools to use the gardens across all disciplines.

Hijacking Curricula

Of course, Waters herself is guilty of nothing more terrible than being a visionary and a woman of tremendous persuasive abilities. It's the state's Department of Education that is to blame for allowing these gardens to hijack the curricula of so many schools. But although garden-based curricula are advanced as a means of redressing a wide spectrum of poverty's ills, the animating spirit behind them is impossible to separate from the haute-bourgeois predilections of the Alice Waters fan club, as best expressed in one of her most off-repeated philosophies: "Gardens help students to learn the pleasure of physical work." Does the immigrant farm worker dream that his child will learn to enjoy manual labor, or that his child will be freed from it? What is the goal of an education, of what we once called "book learning"? These are questions best left unasked when it comes to the gardens.

Hispanics constitute 49 percent of the students in California's public schools. Ever since the state adopted standards-based education (each child must learn a comprehensive set of skills and material) in 1997—coincidentally, at the same moment that garden learning was taking off—a notorious achievement gap has opened between Hispanic and African American students on the one hand, and whites and Asians on the other. Indeed, Hispanic students do particularly poorly at King Middle School. According to the 2009 Federal Accountability Requirements, statewide, more than 39 percent of Latinos are proficient in English and 44 percent in math, but at the King school, those numbers are a dismal 30 percent and 29 percent, respectively. Where do Berkeley's African American and Hispanic middle-schoolers do well? At a gardenless charter school called Cal Prep, where 92 percent of the students are black or Latino, where the focus is on academic achievement, and where test scores have been rising steadily.

The garden-based curriculum has good news for the state's catastrophically underachieving students: a giant team of volunteers is ready to help them. Here is how our garden-loving, home-cooking, recycling superintendent of instruction describes one of the program's principal advantages in the introduction to *A Child's Garden of Standards*, a gargantuan compendium of charts and lesson plans intended to link the beloved method of gardening with the hard-ass objectives of the state standards:

> Some families, particularly those from other countries, may feel uncomfortable when asked to help out at school because their English skills or educational background do not give them a solid classroom footing. For these families, the living classroom of a garden can be a much more inviting environment in which to engage in their children's education.

If this patronizing agenda were promulgated in the Jim Crow South by a white man who was espousing a sharecropping curriculum for African American students, we would see it for what it is: a way of bestowing field work and low expectations on a giant population of students who might become troublesome if they actually got an education.

Hard Question

Here is the essential question we must ask about the school gardens: What evidence do we have that participation in one of these programs—so enthusiastically supported, so uncritically championed—improves a child's chances of doing well on the state tests that will determine his or her future (especially the all-important high-school exit exam) and passing Algebra I, which is becoming the make-or-break class for California high-school students? I have spent many hours poring over the endless research on the positive effects of garden curricula, and in all that time, I have yet to find a single study that suggests classroom gardens help students meet the state standards for English and math. Our kids are working in these gardens with the promise of a better chance at getting an education and a high-school diploma but without one bit of proof that their hard work will result in either. We should remember, by the way, that the California high-school exit exam, which so many are failing, is hardly onerous: it requires a mastery of eighth-grade math (students need to score a mere 55 percent on that portion of the test) and 10th-grade English language and composition (on which they need to score 60 percent or higher). And so I would say this to our state's new child farm laborers: ¡Huelga! Strike!

The ever-evolving rationale behind the school-garden movement mushes together two emotionally stirring ideas: first, that kids will learn by doing, and second, that millions of poor kids have so little access to fruits and vegetables that if they don't spend their school day growing some on campus, they will never get any at all. As a pro-Waters friend observed to me in a recent e-mail, "There's only 7-Eleven in the hood."

As it happens, I live fewer than 20 miles from the most famous American hood, Compton, and on a recent Wednesday morning I drove over there to do a little grocery shopping. The Ralphs was vast, well-lit, bountifully stocked, and possessed of a huge and well-tended produce section. Using my Ralphs card, I bought four ears of corn for a dollar, green grapes and nectarines (both grown in the state, both 49 cents a pound), a pound of fresh tortillas for $1.69, and a half gallon of low-fat milk for $2.19. The staff, California friendly, outnumbered the customers, and the place had the dreamy, lost-in-time feeling that empty American supermarkets often have.

But across Compton Boulevard, it was a different story. Anyone who says that Americans have lost the desire and ability to cook fresh produce has never been to the Superior Super Warehouse in Compton. The produce section—packed with large families, most of them Hispanic—was like a dreamscape of strange and wonderful offerings: tomatillos, giant mangoes, cactus leaves, bunches of beets with their leaves on, chayote squash, red yams, yucca root. An entire string section of chiles: serrano, Anaheim, green, red, yellow. All of it was dirt cheap, as were the bulk beans and rice. Small children stood beside shopping carts with the complacent, slightly dazed look of kids whose mothers are taking care of business.

What we see at Superior Super Warehouse is an example of capitalism doing what it does best: locating a market need (in this case, poor people living in an American inner city who desire a wide variety of fruits and vegetables and who are willing to devote their time and money to acquiring them) and filling it.

But the existence of the monastically quiet Ralphs in Compton reflects something quite different: advocacy. Over the past decade, many well-intentioned factions have made a focused effort to bring supermarkets—and with them, abundant fresh produce—to poor urban areas. Although the battle is far from over, there has been some progress. This seems to me a more sensible approach to getting produce to children than asking the unfortunate tykes to spend precious school hours growing it themselves. Why not make them build the buses that will take them to and from school, or rotate in shifts through the boiler room?

This notion of the school day as an interlude during which children can desperately attempt to cheat ignorance and death by growing the snap peas and zucchini flowers that are the essential building blocks of life comes with a lofty set of ideals. It is a grand vision, which Waters is happy to expand upon to any reporter who takes an interest, and it was described in the following way in last July's *Los Angeles Times*:

Waters says there is a shift in priorities that needs to happen within federal policy to give garden programs longevity. In the 1960s, John F. Kennedy implemented the President's Council on Physical Fitness to instill values of physical fitness. She considers the current prevalence of childhood obesity and early-onset Type 2 diabetes to be signals for immediate action similar to the fitness council.

Well, there's a leap of logic. Waters calls for a new federal program based on an old one, but the new one is necessary only because the old one has obviously failed: American kids are fatter and sicker than ever.

A Simple Truth

Why are obesity and Type 2 diabetes so closely related to low incomes in this country? Surely a good part of the answer lies in a heartrending truth about the experience of poverty that many conservatives (and not a few liberals) either don't know or choose not to know, and it is something I see at my volunteer job in a Los Angeles food bank, where the clients scoop as many candies out of the basket on my desk as I'll let them have (if I didn't set a limit, only the first person would get any) before glumly turning to the matter of filling out their food order form, which offers such basic and unexciting items as tuna, rice, and (yes) fresh fruits and vegetables, often including delicious oranges, pears, and peaches that people with fruit trees donate the day they're picked. The simple truth is expressed clearly by George Orwell in *The Road to Wigan Pier*, his book about the grinding poverty experienced in the North of England in the 1930s:

> The peculiar evil is this: that the less money you have, the less inclined you feel to spend it on wholesome food ... When you are unemployed, which is to say when you are underfed, harassed, bored, and miserable, you don't want to eat dull wholesome food. You want something a little bit "tasty." There is always some cheaply pleasant thing to tempt

you. Let's have a three pennorth of chips! Run out and buy us a two-penny ice cream! Put the kettle on and we'll all have a nice cup of tea . . . Unemployment is an endless misery that has to be palliated.

The suicidal dietary choices of so many poor people are the result of a problem, not the problem itself. The solution lies in an education that will propel students into a higher economic class, where they will live better and therefore eat better.

I started to ask Michael Piscal, founder and CEO of the Inner City Education Foundation Public Schools, which runs 15 successful charter schools in South Los Angeles, what he thought about the Edible Schoolyard and school gardens in general, but he cut me off. "I ignore all those e-mails," he told me bluntly. "Look," he said, when pressed, "there's nothing wrong with kids getting together after school and working on a garden; that's very nice. But when it becomes the center of everything—as it usually does—it's absurd. The only question in education reform that's worth anything is this: What are you doing to prepare these kids for college? If I can get a kid to read Shakespeare and laugh at the right places, I can get him to college. That's all that matters to me."

A Misuse of Time

With the Edible Schoolyard, and the thousands of similar programs, the idea of a school as a venue in which to advance a social agenda has reached rock bottom. This kind of misuse of instructional time began in the Progressive Era, and it has been employed to cheat kids out of thousands of crucial learning hours over the years, so that they might be indoctrinated in whatever the fashionable idea of the moment or the school district might be. One year it's hygiene and another it's anti-Communism; in one city it's safe-sex "outer-course," and in another it's abstinence-only education. (Sixth-graders at King spend an hour and a half each week in the garden or the kitchen—and that doesn't include the time they spend in the classroom, in efforts effective or not, to apply the experiences of planting and cooking to learning the skills and subjects that the state of California mandates must be mastered.) But with these gardens—and their implication that one of the few important things we as a culture have to teach the next generation is what and how to eat—we're mocking one of our most ennobling American ideals. Our children don't get an education because they're lucky, or because we've generously decided to give them one as a special gift. Our children get an education—or should get an education—because they have a right to one. At the very least, shouldn't we ensure that the person who makes her mark on the curricula we teach be someone other than an extremely talented cook with a highly political agenda?

I have spent my life, it seems, in and around schools. For complicated reasons, I attended a score of them, both in the United States and abroad; I taught in Louisiana and Los Angeles for more than a decade; I have volunteered in all sorts of schools, and am now a mother of elementary-school students. I have never seen an entire school system as fundamentally broken and rudderless as the California public schools, a system in which one out of five high-school students drops out before graduation, and in which scarcely 60 percent of the African American and Hispanic students leave school with a diploma. These young people are cast adrift in a $50 billion system in which failure is almost a foregone conclusion.

So why not give these troubled kids a bit of engagement and excitement out in the nourishing gardens, which if nothing else might slim them down and thus extend their lives? Really: How can that hurt?

What Is Essential?

Last October, we lost the greatest educational reformer of the late 20th century, Theodore Sizer, the founder of the Essential

Schools movement, who was brave enough to say that when a school is in crisis, its leaders should strip away every program and resource that is not essential to the mission of schooling. He wrote in his classic 1984 book, *Horace's Compromise*:

> If students have yet to meet the fundamental standards of literacy, numeracy and civic understanding, programs should focus exclusively on these. Some critics will argue that the school must go beyond these subjects to hold the interest of the pupils ... but a fourteen year old who is semi-literate is an adolescent in need of intensive, focused attention.

My state is full of semiliterate 14-year-olds. Let their after-school hours be filled with whatever enriching programs the good volunteers and philanthropic organizations of California care to offer them: club sports, choruses, creative-writing workshops, gardens. But until our kids have a decent chance at mastering the essential skills and knowledge that they will need to graduate from high school, we should devote every resource and every moment of their academic day to helping them realize that life-changing goal. Otherwise, we become complicit—through our best intentions—in an act of theft that will not only contribute to the creation of a permanent, uneducated underclass but will rob that group of the very force necessary to change its fate. The state, which failed these students as children and adolescents, will have to shoulder them in adulthood, for it will have created not a generation of gentleman farmers but one of intellectual sharecroppers, whose fortunes depend on the largesse or political whim of their educated peers.

17

The Quality of Children's Diets Affects Their Brains and Bodies

Alan Greene

Alan Greene is a pediatrician and father of four children. Greene is a past president of the Organic Center and is on the board of directors of Healthy Child Healthy World. He practices medicine in San Francisco, California, and he answers readers' pediatric questions online at www.drgreene.com.

Providing healthy foods and nutritious school lunches to children is about far more than curbing the obesity epidemic. Specific nutrients and additives in food have particular influences on growing children's brains and behavior. A balanced diet rich in organically grown produce is the best formula for producing strong minds and bodies. Parents should become active in ensuring that these guidelines are met not only at home but also in their children's school lunches.

Each day at school, millions of children are faced with a lunch that works against them. Unhealthy versions of French fries, chips, hot dogs, burgers, and pizza fill school cafeterias; high-fat, over-sweetened snacks fill lunch bags brought from home. The crusts and buns of the more popular menu items are likely to be made from over-processed white flour.

Alan Greene, "Brain Food For Your Kids: How Do You Score?" DrGreene.com, January 23, 2007. Copyright © 2007 DrGreene.com. All rights reserved. Reproduced by permission.

The vegetables are likely to be over-cooked and under-appetizing. The beverages are even worse.

Behavior and academic performance are affected by the quantity and quality of the foods we provide children during the school years.

Each day, a growing number of other schoolchildren enjoy delicious lunches that help put them ahead. Their school cafeterias may feature healthy items they will actually choose to eat, while keeping junk foods and beverages out of arm's reach. Or, their parents might send them to school with a tasty, healthy lunch that nourishes their bodies and their brains.

What's on your child's plate today?

It is my strong conviction that children deserve a healthy breakfast to start the school morning right and a healthy school lunch to fuel their growing and their learning. I have come to believe that nutrition plays a key role, by providing them with a critical physiological foundation to help them succeed in school. Behavior and academic performance are affected by the quantity and quality of the foods we provide children during the school years.

From Backyard Gardens to Kindergartens

When I was growing up, my father grew tomatoes in our backyard. These carefully tended, vine-ripened tomatoes were the tastiest I can remember—and it was all thanks to the rich, organically managed soil. All of a tomato plant's growth is made from materials that are available in the soil. This is why plants grown in depleted soils are just not the same. Commercial fertilizers may add back nitrogen and basic minerals, but they cannot replicate the rich spectrum of nourishment in soil that is organically maintained. The plant will just do the best it can with whatever materials are available.

When my daughter Claire was born, she weighed 7 pounds 6 ounces. Today, she is 15 years old and weighs over 100 pounds. All of the materials for Claire's dramatic growth have come from the food she has eaten. Like the tomato plant, my daughter's body does the best it can with what's available.

Food is the building block for every part of a child's body, from bones and skin and muscles to organs, including the brain and its complex, ever growing network of neural connections. Children's bodies are very forgiving—but why not offer them the best building blocks during the school years? And why not protect them from chemicals and junk ingredients in what they eat and drink, or from foods that have the nourishment processed out of them?

Brain Building

Today in the United States, 1 in 6 children suffers from a disability that affects their behavior, memory, or ability to learn. More than $80 billion dollars are spent each year to treat neurodevelopmental disorders. Diagnoses of Attention Deficit Hyperactivity Disorder (ADHD) alone up are up 250% since 1990. How much of a role does modern food play in this increase?

Growing children quite literally are what they eat.

Children's brains are built differently depending on what they are fed when they are rapidly growing. Healthy brains are about 60% structural fat (not like the flabby fat found elsewhere in the body). As the brain grows, it selects building blocks from among the fatty acids available in what the child eats. The most prevalent structural fat in the brain is DHA (docosahexaenoic acid), one of the omega 3 fatty acids. DHA is also a major structural component of the retina of the eye.

A large number of studies have suggested that low DHA levels are associated with problems with intelligence, vision, and behavior.

DHA is the most prevalent long chain fatty acid in human breast milk, which suggests that it's intended for babies to consume a lot of it. Studies have shown that babies who have not gotten DHA in their diets have significantly less of it in their brains than those who have.

My point here is not about the superiority of breast milk, but that growing children quite literally are what they eat. When you think about this, you begin to feel differently about "cheap" food.

How Our Food Is Grown

We've established that kids develop differently depending on how they are nourished. Now let's return to how the food they eat is, in turn, affected by what materials are available to grow it.

For instance, cheese, milk, and meat can provide high levels of DHA and other omega 3's (as well as providing high levels vitamin E and beta carotene) if it's produced from pasture-fed organic cows, but not from grain-fed confinement cows. Simply put, fresh grass provides the building blocks for a different quality of product.

Iron

Iron is another nutrient that is essential to optimal brain function. Here's a very interesting study reported in the December 2004 *Archives of Pediatrics and Adolescent Medicine*—the first to connect children's iron levels and ADHD.

ADHD has increasingly affected school classrooms in recent years. Between March 2002 and June 2003, 110 children from a school district in Paris, France were referred to a university hospital to be evaluated for school-related problems. Researchers analyzed blood samples from the 53 of these children who met the diagnostic criteria for ADHD, and from 27 of the children who did not. The average ferritin (iron) level in the non-ADHD kids was normal, but the average level in the children with ADHD was about half that of the other children. Fully 84% of the children with ADHD were iron deficient. And the lower the iron levels, the worse the ADHD symptoms—worse hyperactivity, worse oppositional behavior, and worse cognitive scores.

The stunning part of this study was that *none of the children had iron levels low enough to indicate anemia.* The iron deficiency was subtle enough that all tested normal on the hemoglobin or hematocrit blood tests used in doctors' offices to screen for iron problems. I suspect that inadequate iron in the diet is also affecting the attention, focus, and activity of many children who don't meet the full definition of ADHD.

When other researchers fed appropriate iron to children with ADHD, their test scores and ADHD symptoms improved.

We know from a large body of previous research that school-aged children who are iron deficient don't learn as well. School performance is worse; memory is weakened. ADHD is more often seen in boys, but girls are also seriously affected by low iron. Today in the U.S., we are seeing that iron deficiency impacts intellectual growth in as many as 1 in 6 girls sometime in their school careers. Other studies have shown that teen girls with low iron are more than twice as likely to score below average in math achievement tests as are similar girls with normal iron status—even if they have no signs of anemia.

The amount of iron children get from foods depends not just on what types of food they choose, but on how that food is grown. Recent evidence has shown that conventional, chemical farming has resulted in depleted nutrients in common food crops. Levels of vitamins and minerals (including iron) have fallen over the last fifty years, as this type of agriculture prevailed.

Antioxidants

Kids need more than isolated, individual nutrients to boost their brains and school performance. There are big-picture benefits to eating a balanced diet rich in fruits and vegetables, whole grains, and fiber. Antioxidants include a large variety of compounds found in a large variety of whole foods. Antioxidants in foods have been linked to improved memory and brain function.

Even in the same food, antioxidant levels can vary depending on how the food is grown. Organic foods, on average, are about 30% higher in antioxidants than are their non-organic counterparts. That means each organic serving may be packed with more valuable nutrients. Talk about extra credit!

Avoid Organophosphates

Organophosphates are the most commonly used insecticides in conventional, chemical agriculture. These chemicals act as nerve agents, and have been linked to neurodevelopmental problems. Organically-grown foods are produced without the use of toxic pesticides such as organophosphates. Choosing organic foods for children can immediately and significantly decrease their exposure to organophosphate pesticides. That's good protection for the developing brain—it's elementary.

Some are afraid that school children would have to eat unfamiliar or unappetizing foods in order to make a difference. Not so! A February 2006 study conducted by Dr. Chensheng Lu and colleagues demonstrated an immediate and dramatic ability to reduce organophosphate pesticide exposure by making *simple* diet changes in elementary school children.

The researchers conducted this study with typical suburban children. They collected morning and evening urine samples daily from each child. Pesticide breakdown products appeared routinely in the urine samples.

Then the researchers made a simple change: the elementary school kids began eating organic versions of whatever they were eating before. For example, if they typically ate apples, now they got organic apples. Only if there was a simple organic substitution available for what the kids were already eating, did they make a switch. The kids didn't have to learn to like any new foods.

Within 24 hours, pesticide breakdown products found in the urine plummeted! They continued this way for five days, with clean urine samples morning and night. Then the kids went back to their typical diets. The organic foods were taken away. And immediately the pesticides returned. These elementary school children went back to a chronic low-level exposure to organophosphate pesticides from the diet.

Additives

Researchers at the University of Southampton studied over 1800 three-year-old children, some with and some without ADHD, some with and some without allergies. After initial behavioral testing, all of the children got one week of a diet without any artificial food colorings and without any chemical preservatives. The children's behavior measurably improved during this week. But was this from the extra attention, from eating more fruits and vegetables, or from the absence of the preservatives and artificial colors?

To answer this question, the researchers continued the diet, but gave the children disguised drinks containing either a mixture of artificial colorings and the preservative benzoate, or similarly colored drinks from natural, food sources. The weeks that children got the hidden chemicals, their behavior was substantially worse. This held true whether or not they had been diagnosed with hyperactivity, and whether or not they had tested positive for allergies—good news for parents everywhere!

Removing artificial colors and preservatives from the diet was dramatically effective at reducing hyperactivity—somewhere between the effectiveness of clonidine and Ritalin, two prescription ADHD drugs. How much better to support children's mood and behavior with healthy food, than with drugs! Some children may still need medicine, but with a healthy diet, we may be able to use lower doses. And it stands to reason that this diet would be better for all children, whether or not they have behavior problems.

Refined Sugars and Flours

Food processing can have other negative effects on kids' brains. In the 1800s the average American consumed 12 pounds of sugar per year. Due to the overwhelming success of the refined-food industry, however, by 1975 sugar consumption had jumped 1000% to 118 pounds per capita, and continued increasing to an average of 137.5 pounds for every man, woman, and child by 1990.

Where are all these sugars coming from? It's not just cookies, candies, and other sweet treats! Sugars—and more recently, high fructose corn syrup—show up on an astonishing variety of food labels, and high on the list of ingredients in the sweetened beverages that kids guzzle. They are ubiquitous in many convenience foods and fast foods, and you will find them in much of the processed food served in school lunches.

The effect of sugar intake is a hotly debated topic in pediatrics. Parents and educators often contend that sugar and other carbohydrate ingestion can dramatically impact children's behavior, activity and attention. However, physicians looking at controlled studies of sugar intake do not find hypoglycemia or other blood sugar abnormalities in the children who are consuming large amounts of sugar.

The *Journal of Pediatrics* reported that there is a more pronounced response to a glucose load in children than in adults. In children, hypoglycemia-like symptoms (including shakiness, sweating, and altered thinking and behavior) may occur at a blood sugar level that would not be considered hypoglycemic. The authors reason that the problem is not sugar, per se, but highly refined sugars and carbohydrates, which enter the bloodstream quickly and produce more rapid fluctuations in blood glucose levels.

Serving a breakfast with complex carbohydrates (like oatmeal, shredded wheat, berries, bananas, or whole-grain pancakes) and packing a lunch with delicious fiber-containing treats (such as whole-grain breads and fresh fruit) will help keep your child's adrenaline levels more constant, which may increase their ability to pay attention in school.

Overcooking

When foods are cooked, their nutrient profile changes. For instance, overcooking can destroy beta-carotene, an important antioxidant. Overcooked carrots have significantly lower antioxidants overall than do raw or gently cooked carrots. The same is true for broccoli and asparagus. Baked or boiled russet potatoes have higher nutrient levels than do raw potatoes—but frying the potatoes destroys important nutrients. Peeling some foods (such as apples, potatoes, or cucumbers) can also decrease antioxidant power.

School Fuel

Kids' brains are high-performance engines, and if we want them to do their best in school, we need to provide them with clean, high-quality fuel. For growing children this means a balanced diet of delicious whole foods, grown in a nutrition-enhancing way without toxic pesticides, and prepared in an appealing manner that also preserves nutrients.

As a pediatrician, it is my strong conviction that kids need and deserve a healthy breakfast before school. Several studies have shown that a good breakfast can result in better academic performance in the classroom and higher standardized test scores in math, reading, and vocabulary.

And the need for quality food doesn't stop when . . . kids leave the house in the morning. Every child deserves to have a balanced, nutritious lunch at school, every day. Organic dairy products, proteins (beans, nuts, eggs, or lean meat), whole grains and fresh fruit and vegetables are all recommended parts of the school lunch curriculum. . . .

Solid science has shown that food affects kids memory, attention, and cognitive skills. Even whether or not they eat breakfast changes their test scores. What they eat, how their food is grown, and how their food is processed can all help their brains to operate at their very best. . . .

How Much Does a Child Need Each Day?

Kids can benefit from dietary improvements at any age. Quality foods make a difference when they are young, and their brains are growing most rapidly. It also makes a huge difference for teens, whose brains are restructuring for adult life.

For most kids, about 80% of adult height is gained before 6th grade is over, but the need for quality nutrition doesn't stop there. About 20% of adult height and 50% of adult weight are gained during adolescence. Most boys double their lean body mass between the ages of 10 and 17. Because growth and change is so rapid during this period, the requirements for all nutrients increase.

You can use these guidelines to help make nutritious choices and create balanced meals. . . . And remember that organic foods may provide a nutrition bonus from healthy mineral content, higher antioxidant content, as well as lowering . . . [a] child's exposure to developmentally disruptive pesticides. So whenever possible, make it organic!

Girls
* Organic beans, nuts, eggs, or lean meats

ages 4–8
Whole grains—4 oz
Vegetables—1 cup
Fruits—1.5 cups
Protein*—3 oz
Milk**—2 cups
ages 9–13
Whole grains—5 oz
Vegetables—2 cups
Fruits—1.5 cups
Protein*—5 oz
Milk**—3 cups
ages 14–18
Whole grains—6 oz
Vegetables—2.5 cups
Fruits—1.5 cups
Protein*—5 oz
Milk**—3 cups

Boys
** Organic milk, other dairy, or other source of calcium and protein

ages 4–8
Whole grains—5 oz
Vegetables—1.5 cups
Fruits—1.5 cups
Protein*—4 oz
Milk**—2 cups
ages 9–13
Whole grains—6 oz
Vegetables—2.5 cups
Fruits—1.5 cups
Protein*—5 oz
Milk**—3 cups
ages 14–18
Whole grains—7 oz
Vegetables—3 cups
Fruits—2 cups
Protein*—6 oz
Milk*—3 cups

Organizations to Contact

The editors have compiled the following list of organizations concerned with the issues debated in this book. The descriptions are derived from materials provided by the organizations. All have publications or information available for interested readers. The list was compiled on the date of publication of the present volume; the information provided here may change. Readers need to remember that many organizations take several weeks or longer to respond to inquiries.

Campaign for a Commercial-Free Childhood (CCFC)
NonProfit Center, 89 South St., #404, Boston, MA 02111
(857) 241-2028 • fax: (617) 737-1585
e-mail: ccfc@commercialfreechildhood.org
website: www.commercialfreechildhood.org

Founded in 2000, the Campaign for a Commercial-Free Childhood's mission is to "reclaim childhood from corporate marketers." Through advocacy and grass-roots organizing, it works to limit children's exploitation through commercial culture. Among its many initiatives, the CCFC actively discourages marketing in schools, including vending machines and other forms of food marketing. The organization's website offers fact sheets, calls to actions, and links to recent news stories.

Center for Science in the Public Interest (CSPI)
1875 Connecticut Ave. NW, Washington, DC 20009
(202) 332-9110 • fax: (202) 265-4954
e-mail: cspinews@cspinet.org
website: www.cspinet.org

The Center for Science in the Public Interest is a consumer advocacy group devoted to funding public policy initiatives as well as scientific research. The organization also works to improve consumer awareness of health and nutrition issues, in large part through a subscription-based magazine (portions of which are available for free online), *Nutrition Action Healthletter*, which includes healthy recipes as well as regular features such as "Right Stuff vs. Food Porn" and analyses of menus at popular restaurants. CSPI's website has a section on "School Foods," which includes a quiz to test users' knowledge of the issue as well as specific suggestions for improving school lunches, snacks, celebrations, and reward programs.

Chez Panisse Foundation

1517 Shattuck Ave., Berkeley, CA   94709
(510) 843-3811 • fax: (510) 843-3880
e-mail: info@chezpanissefoundation.org
website: www.chezpanissefoundation.org

According to its website, the Chez Panisse Foundation "envisions a school curriculum and school lunch program where growing, cooking, and sharing food at the table gives students the knowledge and values to build a humane and sustainable future." The organization advocates for school lunch reform, in particular the Edible Schoolyard initiative, which involves schoolchildren in growing their own food. The foundation's website offers many publications for sale for educators and parents.

Farm to School

Urban and Environmental Policy Institute, Occidental College, 1600 Campus Rd., MS-M1, Los Angeles, CA   90041
website: www.farmtoschool.org

Sponsored by the Urban and Environmental Policy Institute at Occidental College, Farm to School's objective is to connect K-12 schools with local farms with the goal of creating sustainable local school food programs. Now with programs in all fifty states, Farm to School is overseen by eight regional coordinators who form a national Farm to School network. They sponsor many local and national events aimed at educating educators, consumers, and administrators about the benefits of locally grown, sustainably produced foods for farmers and for kids. The organization's website offers many resources, including educational online videos.

Green Schools Initiative

2150 Allston Way, Suite 460, Berkeley, CA   94704
(510) 525-1026
e-mail: info@greenschools.net
website: www.greenschools.net

For the Green Schools Initiative, healthy school lunches are just one facet of an overall approach to healthy, green living at school. Other goals include improving air quality using natural light, saving energy, creating green schoolyards, and teaching stewardship of the environment. The initiative's website profiles some schools following this model and offers a set of seven steps schools can follow to easily improve their environments. It also includes lists of green school products and recommended environmentally friendly industrial cleaners schools can use to keep their environments safe.

Grocery Manufacturers Association

1350 I St., Washington, DC   20005
website: www.grmaonline.org

The Grocery Manufacturers Association is the largest trade association for companies making food and beverage products. It channels political contributions, lobbies, and conducts public relations on behalf of its member corporations, which include such huge companies as Kraft Foods and Pepsi. The association's website provides information about the association's public policy regarding school nutrition and food marketing.

Healthy Child Healthy World

12300 Wilshire Blvd., Suite 320, Los Angeles, CA   90025
(310) 820-2030 • fax: (310) 820-2070
website: www.healthychild.org

Healthy Child Healthy World is a nonprofit organization dedicated to helping both children and the environment by limiting children's exposure to harmful chemicals. The organization believes that by cutting back on these chemicals and pesticides, many diseases could be eliminated or their effects greatly diminished. The organization was founded by a couple who lost their young child to a rare form of cancer that could, perhaps, have been been caused by exposure to harmful chemicals. The organization's website promotes a DVD outlining steps homes, day care centers, and schools can take to provide safer environments for children as well as a parenting book and free fact sheets.

Healthy School Lunches
5100 Wisconsin Ave. NW, Suite 400
Washington, DC   20016-4131
(202) 686-2210 • fax: (202) 686-2216
e-mail: hschoollunches@pcrm.org
website: www.healthyschoollunches.org

Sponsored by the Physicians Committee for Responsible Medicine, Healthy School Lunches is committed to advocating for healthier school lunch programs in schools. In particular, the group aims to reduce saturated fat in the lunches served at schools and to improve the amount of plant-based foods served at school. The organization's website issues an annual report card on lunch programs at some of the country's largest school districts and offers many other resources, including sample vegetarian menus, nutrition basics, and profiles of schools making a difference.

Organic Consumers Association
6771 S Silver Hill Dr., Finland, MN   55603
(218) 226-4164
website: www.organicconsumers.org/afc.cfm

The Organic Consumers Association sponsors the initiative "Appetite for Change." The initiative's goals are to "Stop spraying toxic pesticides on school property, playgrounds and in buildings, and convert to integrated pest management practices; kick junk foods and junk food ads out of our schools; start converting school lunches to healthier menus . . . teach kids about healthy food choices and sustainable agriculture through school garden projects and curriculum materials." The organization's website offers links to current news stories, action alerts, and links to other relevant organizations.

Parents Against Junk Food

PO Box 470689, Brookline, MA 02447
e-mail: PAJF@parentsagainstjunkfood.org
website: www.parentsagainstjunkfood.org

Parents Against Junk Food has a straightforward mission: "Stop the sale of junk food in America's schools." Members receive a free e-newsletter and are encouraged to help support anti-junk food legislation in their states. The organization's website includes links to relevant news stories as well as a "Junk Food Hall of Shame," highlighting the poor nutritional choices available to children in America's schools.

Yale Rudd Center for Food Policy and Obesity

PO Box 208369, New Haven, CT 06520-8369
(203) 432-6700
e-mail: andrea.wilson@yale.edu
website: www.yaleruddcenter.org

The Yale Rudd Center for Food Policy and Obesity seeks to "improve the world's diet, prevent obesity, and reduce weight stigma" through a combination of supporting scientific research and lobbying to improve public policy surrounding these issues. The center's website includes a blog, a collection of podcasts featuring noted experts, and links to the organization's presence on various social media networks. The website also includes the center's own policy briefs and reports as well as links to recent publications about nutrition, food marketing, and obesity.

Bibliography

Books

Hank Cardello	*Stuffed: An Insider's Look at Who's (Really) Making America Fat.* New York: Ecco, 2009.
Ann Cooper	*Lunch Lessons: Changing the Way We Feed Our Children.* New York: Harper, 2007.
Julie Lautenschlager	*Food Fight! The Battle over the American Lunch in Schools and the Workplace.* Jefferson, NC: McFarland & Co., 2006.
Susan Levine	*School Lunch Politics: The Surprising History of America's Favorite Welfare Program.* Princeton, NJ: Princeton University Press, 2010.
Joseph Mercola	*Generation XL: Raising Healthy, Intelligent Kids in a High-Tech, Junk-Food World.* Nashville, TN: Thomas Nelson, 2007.
Marion Nestle	*What to Eat: An Aisle-by-Aisle Guide to Savvy Food Choices and Good Eating.* New York: North Point Press, 2006.
Janet Poppendieck	*Free for All: Fixing School Food in America.* Berkeley, CA: University of California Press, 2010.

Michele Simon *Appetite for Profit: How the Food Industry Undermines Our Health and How to Fight Back.* New York: Nation Books, 2006.

Michael K. Stone *Smart by Nature: Schooling for Sustainability.* Healdsburg, CA: Watershed Media, 2009.

Alice Waters *Edible Schoolyard: A Universal Idea.* San Francisco: Chronicle Books, 2008.

Walter C. Willett *Eat, Drink and Be Healthy: The Harvard Medical School Guide to Healthy Eating.* New York: Free Press, 2005.

Periodicals

Burkhard Bilger "The Lunchroom Rebellion," *The New Yorker*, September 4, 2006.

Sheila Fleischhacker "Food Fight: The Battle over Redefining Competitive Foods," *Journal of School Health*, March 2007.

Ellen J. Fried and Michele Simon "The Competitive Food Conundrum: Can Government Regulations Improve School Food?" *Duke Law Journal*, April 2007.

Corbett Grainger, Benjamin Senauer, and C. Ford Runge "Nutritional Improvements and Student Food Choices in a School Lunch Program," *Journal of Consumer Affairs*, Winter 2007.

Michael Harms — "Big Macs and Healthy Teens? Exploring Fast Food as Part of a Healthy Adolescent Lifestyle," *Science Scope*, March 2009.

Peter Hinrichs — "The Effects of the National School Lunch Program on Education and Health," *Journal of Policy Analysis and Management*, Summer 2010.

Stephanie Johns — "The Feud over Food: The Truth about the School Lunch Wars," *District Administration*, January 2010.

Corby Kummer — "Fixing Lunch," *The Atlantic*, May 22, 2009.

Katharine Quarmby — "Grease Is the Word," *The New Statesman*, February 20, 2006.

Meabh Ritchie — "Naked Lunch Box," *Times Educational Supplement*, March 26, 2010.

Diane Whitmore Schanzebach — "Do School Lunches Contribute to Childhood Obesity?" *Journal of Human Resources*, Summer 2009.

Anastasia M. Snelling, Casey Korba, and Alyvia Burkey — "The National School Lunch and Competitive Food Offerings and Purchasing Behaviors of High School Students," *Journal of School Health*, December 2007.

Mary Story, Karen M. Kaphingst, and Simone French — "The Role of Schools in Obesity Prevention," *The Future of Children*, Spring 2006.

Marilyn Swanson   "Eating Healthier in School," *Food Technology*, September 2006.

Deborah Lau   "Let Them Eat Kale: With America's
Whelan   Kids in Danger of Becoming Obese,
                     a Growing Number of Schools Are
                     Thinking Outside the Lunchbox,"
                     School Library Journal, June 2008.

Index

L

Lakeview Elementary School, 76
Lee, Dick, 61
"Let's Move" anti-obesity program, 7, 16–17, 19, 33–34
Little Debbie marshmallow treats, 59
Los Angeles Times article, 86, 90
Lu, Chensheng, 100

M

Majoras, Deborah Platt (FTC Chairman), 30
Martin Luther King Jr. Middle School (Berkeley), 77–78, 85, 87
Maynard, Althesia, 23, 24
McDonald's Happy Meals, 24–25
McGinnis, Michael, 30
McKenna, Mary, 80
McNamee, Thomas, 84
McNerthney, Casey, 59–64
Medical opposition to junk food, 11–12
Milk, flavored/sugar-filled, 18–19
Murphy, Hardy, 47
Mushroom risotto, 7

N

Nacho entrees, 45
Naperville Central High School, 48
National School Lunch Program (USDA), 7–8, 46, 49
Nestle, Marion, 33–36
"A New Crop of School Gardens" *(Los Angeles Times)*, 86
Nielsen, Steve, 63

North Community High School (Minnesota), 39
Norton, Eleanor Holmes, 30–31
Nutrition and student bodies, 95–105
  additives, 101–102
  antioxidants, 100
  brain building, 97–98
  daily requirements, 104–105
  food for fuel for school, 103–104
  iron, 98–99
  organophosphate avoidance, 100–101
  overcooking food, 103
  refined sugars and flours, 102–103

O

Obama, Barack
  anti-childhood obesity task force, 34
  economic funding goals, 47
  healthy school program promotion, 42
  increased spending recommendations, 22
Obama, Michelle
  anti-obesity campaigns, 7, 16–17, 19, 33
  healthier school goals, 41–43
  "healthy eating event," 42
  opposition to campaigns of, 35
  promotion of vegetables, 19
  reaching out to business groups, 34–35
  See also "Let's Move" anti-obesity program
Obama, Sasha and Malia, 42